Problem/Solution

A REFERENCE FOR ESL WRITERS

PATRICIA BYRD
Georgia State University

BEVERLY BENSON
DeKalb College

Heinle & Heinle Publishers
A Division of Wadsworth, Inc.
20 Park Plaza, Boston, MA 02116 U.S.A.

The publication of *Problem/Solution: A Reference for ESL Writers* was directed by the members of the Global Innovations Team at Heinle & Heinle:

David C. Lee, Editorial Director
John F. McHugh, Marketing Development Director
Gabrielle B. McDonald, Production Editor

Also participating in the publication of this program were:

Publisher: Stanley J. Galek
Editorial Production Manager: Elizabeth Holthaus
Project Manager: Stacey Sawyer, Sawyer & Williams
Assistant Editor: Kenneth Mattsson
Associate Marketing Manager: Donna Hamilton
Production Assistant: Maryellen Eschmann
Manufacturing Coordinator: Mary Beth Hennebury
Interior Designer: Rogondino Associates
Cover Illustrator and Designer: Maureen Lauren

Heinle & Heinle Publishers is a division of Wadsworth, Inc.

Manufactured in the United States of America

Library of Congress Cataloging in Publication Data

Byrd, Patricia.
   Problem/solution : a reference for ESL writers / by Patricia Byrd and Beverly Benson.
     p.   cm.
   Includes index.
   ISBN 0-8384-4125-4
   1. English language—Textbooks for foreign speakers. 2. English language—
Composition and exercises. 3. English language—Grammar. I. Benson, Beverly.
II. Title.
PE1128.B869   1993
428.2′4—dc20
                                               93-38194
                                                    CIP

10 9 8 7 6 5 4 3 2 1

Contents

I. GRAMMAR POINTS

II. PUNCTUATION

Contents

*	An asterisk is placed at the beginning of a sentence that has a grammatical error.	*He did not do the homeworks.
<u>underlining</u>	Single underlining indicates the subject of a sentence. Double underlining marks the verb.	<u>All college courses</u> should increase a student's ability to think.
Times Roman print	This style of print is used for explanations.	An apostrophe is added to words for two major purposes: to indicate possessive meaning and to mark contractions.
Courier print	This style of print is used for examples.	Maria will study chemistry next quarter.
italic print	Italic print is used to indicate terminology the first time that a special term is used. Words given as examples inside an explanation will be in italic print. Also, lists of words are given in italic print.	*Subject-verb agreement* is a relationship between a subject and a verb. The subject requires a particular form for the verb.
bold print	Bold print is used to mark parts of examples to point out the area being discussed in the text.	error highlighted in bold print *He **will can** study chemistry next quarter.

★	A star is used to mark a sentence with a punctuation error. Usually such sentences are grammatically correct but do not meet the stylistic standards of formal academic writing.	★I believe, she will graduate next year.
☛	A pointing hand marks all practice materials.	☛ **Practice 1**
☹	A frowning face marks materials that are grammatically correct but have some problem with meaning or style.	☹ If people wear expensive clothes, they must be rich.
✔	A check mark is used to indicate a cross-reference to materials on a related topic.	✔40. Fragments

The Focus on Editing graphic on p. ix covers 12 common ESL errors divided into three sections: the ranking (1 to 12) places the most serious errors, the most important errors, at the top.

The first section contains the four most serious errors. These errors affect the reader's ability to understand the ideas in a paper. In their study of written English, students should focus on these topics first.

The middle section contains less serious but also important errors that usually do not cause misunderstanding. They affect parts of sentences, and they may be distracting. These errors are not generally as rule-bound as others and take students additional time listening to and reading in English before improvement usually occurs.

The three errors in the third section can be handled at the last stage of writing. Knowledge of comma and capitalization rules and a good dictionary will be helpful here.

It is important to remember that writing problems are not isolated from each other and that distinctions among them are not always clear. However, the Focus on Editing chart is designed to help students make decisions about how to improve their own written English and about how to organize their learning process by focusing on the most serious problems first.

Improving the Grammar of Written English: The Editing Process, Improving the Grammar of Written English: The Handbook, and *Applied English Grammar* further develop the connection between editing skills and improved accuracy and fluency in written English.

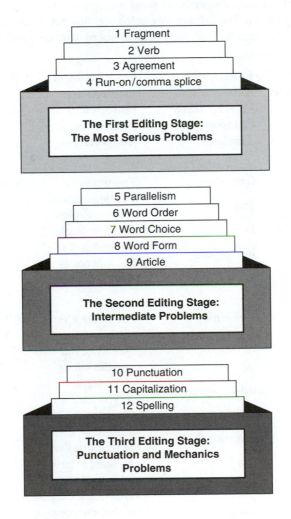

EDITING KEY

Composition teachers generally use some system to mark problems on student papers. Some teachers will use a system like that shown in the Focus on Editing chart. In these systems, the teachers use numbers to identify particular problems. For example, "1" written near a sentence indicates that the sentence is a fragment (an incomplete sentence). Other teachers write words or abbreviations to indicate problems. These teachers will write the word *fragment* or the abbreviation *frag* near an incomplete sentence. The Editing Key helps you find help in *Problem/Solution* to fit the particular problem that has been pointed out by your composition teachers.

Editing by the Numbers Used in Focus on Editing	Editing with Abbreviations Used by Some Composition Teachers	Explanation of the Problem Indicated by the Number or Abbreviation	*Problem/Solution* Unit to Turn to for Help with This Problem
1	fragment frag f incomplete inc	You wrote a fragment rather than a complete sentence. Some required part of the sentence is missing.	✔40. Fragments
2a	verb tense vb vt tense verb conditional con modal passive pass	You wrote a verb that is in the wrong tense. Or, you used the wrong modal form. Or, you used a passive sentence incorrectly. Check the meaning that you want to have, and then study the verbs that are used for that meaning.	✔Unit 21 and Units 25–36

Editing Key

2b	verb form vb vf verb	You spelled a verb wrong.	✔27. Irregular Verbs ✔32. Past Time Writing ✔33. Present Time Writing
3a	noun plural num pl +s	You wrote the wrong form for a plural noun. Perhaps you left off the final +s.	✔ 7. Noncount Nouns ✔ 9. Irregular Plural Nouns ✔10. Plural and Singular Forms: Consistency of Use in Writing
3b	subject-verb agreement sva sv agreement	You wrote the wrong form of the subject or the verb for subject-verb agreement.	✔2. Subject-Verb Agreement
3c	noun-pronoun agreement pronoun agreement npa noun-pronoun np pronoun	You used the wrong pronoun form; it does not agree with the noun that it refers to.	✔1. Noun-Pronoun Agreement
4	run-on sentence run-on ro	If the problem is a "run-on" sentence, you wrote a compound sentence with a coordinating conjunction and left out the comma.	✔41. Run-On Sentences

Editing Key

5	commas splice cs splice	If the problem is a "comma splice," you wrote a comma to make a compound sentence but have not used a coordinating conjunction.	✔38. Comma Splices
6	parallel structure parallel // not parallel	There are two possible errors that you could have made: (1) You had a problem with grammatical parallelism—the forms were not the same grammatically. (2) You had a logical problem—the forms were not of the same meaning.	✔20. Grammatical and Logical Parallelism
7	word order wo awk k	You placed some part of a sentence in the wrong position.	✔15. Compound Sentences ✔22. Complex Sentences and Sentence Combining ✔23. Subordinating Conjunctions and Types of Subordination

7	word choice wc wrong word ww awk choice diction d usage u	You selected a word that is not correct for the meaning or the grammar that you need to use.	✔24. Making Transitions and Using Transition Words
8	word form wf word	You used the wrong form of a word.	✔ 9. Irregular Plural Nouns ✔10. Plural and Singular Forms: Consistency of Use in Writing ✔27. Irregular Verbs
9	article art	You selected the wrong article for the noun meaning that you need. Or, you left out an article when one is required for the meaning that you need.	✔Units 3–11

10a	punctuation punct pun p	You made a punctuation error. Some teachers will use this number or word for all types of punctuation errors.	✔Units 37–42
10b	comma c ,	You made an error with a comma. Either you left one out, or you put one in the wrong place.	✔37. Commas ✔38. Comma Splices ✔41. Run-On Sentences
10c	other punctuation types ; semicolon	Some teachers are more specific about punctuation errors and will give particular words or numbers for particular errors.	✔Units 37–42
12	spelling sp spell	You spelled a word incorrectly.	✔ 9. Irregular Plural Nouns ✔27. Irregular Verbs

Editing Key

Symbol	Meaning	Example
℘	delete or remove a word or group of words	I went to the (the) computer lab early on Saturday morning.
¶	indent to make a new paragraph at the point where the symbol is placed	**Winning the Lottery** I am a college student. My daily life has been more or less a routine for the past two years. All week long, I either attend classes or go to work. I cannot say that I hate my present routine, but if I won a million dollars I would certainly welcome a few changes in my present lifestyle. ¶ The first change would be to stop waiting for the money coming from home that I never receive on time. The late arrival of my living expenses has been a problem for the past two years. I am sure that a million dollars would relieve that problem.
ss	sentence structure problem	*H104 is one of the smallest classroom in our *ss* campus that hold 12 students.
What ? ?	meaning or handwriting not clear	Jana College Student

Additional Symbols Used in Editing

Information About *Problem/Solution*

I. Strategic Competence. Communicative competence involves four areas: (1) linguistic competence, (2) discourse competence, (3) sociolinguistic competence, and (4) strategic competence. The last of these involves learning strategies for dealing with miscommunication as well as strategies for improving communication. *Problem/Solution* is designed to help students improve their strategic competence by providing them with materials through which they can repair their errors and expand their knowledge of particular areas of written English grammar.

     Problem/Solution is for the student writer who needs fast, to-the-point, and easy-to-find information about particularly troublesome areas of the grammar of written academic English. The coverage is focused on problem areas rather than providing a general presentation of English grammar. *Problem/Solution* is intended as a handbook to complement or supplement texts that provide instruction in the writing of academic English.

II. Accurate Fluency and Fluent Accuracy. A major goal of this reference book is to help ESL and EFL writers to become both more accurate and more fluent in their academic writing. Through improved knowledge of English and through use of the information and the examples in this book during revisions of papers, students can learn to write more accurately. At the same time, students can develop more skill and greater confidence in their writing so that they can write with more ease and fluency.

III. Audience. The book is for high-intermediate to advanced ESL/EFL students, especially those who are taking writing courses in ESL/EFL programs, in Developmental Studies programs, and in English departments. *Problem/Solution* is also planned for students working in writing labs to improve their accurate fluency.

     We expect that many teachers of ESL and of English composition will use the text to guide students to information that can help with particular problems in English grammar. In addition, some teachers might find *Problem/Solution* of use for themselves as a guide to the kinds of problems their students are experiencing.

IV. Overall Organization. The difficulty for students in using a grammar handbook is finding the right entry for the information that they need. Since many ESL students seem to be comfortable with dictionary format, the materials have been divided into short units that are arranged in alphabetical order.

     An Answer Key to selected items is provided at the end of this book. Generally, answers are provided to every other question so that students can understand how a particular exercise is to be done. This system provides students with support for independent study and yet prevents their becoming so dependent on the Answer Key that they do not have the experience of attempting to work out the answers for themselves.

An Editing Key (p. x) helps students find information based on editing symbols used by composition teachers. A student can look for an editing symbol and then quickly find the relevant sections of *Problem/Solution*. Teachers, too, can use the Editing Key to point students to materials that can help with particular problems.

A section of cross-references is provided at the end of each unit to guide users to other related materials.

V. Organization of Each Unit. Typically, a unit is organized into four parts: general information, "problem" information, practice activities, and cross-references. The general information about the topic has explanations on the left and examples on the right. This section is often followed by a "problem" section in which particular problem areas are illustrated. "Problems" are always divided into three sections: problem, solution, and revision.

This presentation provides students with two ways of thinking about their own English grammar. They can learn new information about English or clarify their understanding of those areas. In addition, students can see typical problems and learn about ways to revise sentences containing those errors. This presentation is based on the dual aspects of the Editing Process: (1) first, a writer must recognize that a problem exists. (2) Second, the writer must have some strategies for correcting the problem.

VI. Format. The materials are in table format because of student preference for that style. Students seem to find it easier to separate examples from explanations when the materials are in separate boxes. To make materials even easier to read, different styles of tables are used in *Problem/Solution* for different types of material. Informational tables that give general explanations are in a different style from "problem" tables so that users can more easily find material that they are seeking.

In addition, material has been divided into chunks that are easy for students to read and understand when they are working on their own without support from a teacher. For example, rather than having a large section on articles and nouns, that content has been divided into nine units, each containing a subsection of the larger content. Students can study as much of the material as they need or can handle at a particular time.

VII. How the Book Can Be Used by Students for Different Purposes. There are three major reasons that a student will use *Problem/Solution*. First, a teacher will find that a student has trouble with a particular area of grammar and will direct the student to study particular sections. That is, the teacher will help the student make some choices and will be available to discuss the materials if the student has questions.

In the second situation, a teacher will comment that the student has trouble with verbs or fragments or parallelism and "needs to do something about it." That is, the student is going to be on her/his own to try to figure out what has gone wrong and what to do to avoid that particular problem in the future. This unfortunate reality is true for many students; we need to find ways to help those students get to the right information as easily as possible.

There might be a third situation: some writers seek information because they themselves want to improve the accuracy of their written English. These writers, too, will find in *Problem/Solution* a book that is easy to use and is focused on information that is of help with particular problems in the grammar of written English.

Acknowledgments

It is our pleasure to thank several friends and colleagues who helped make *Problem/Solution* possible by contributing their encouragement, energy, ideas, and time. We are indebted to teachers and students at Georgia State University and DeKalb College for their help and support during the writing and field testing of this text and for their writing samples used as models for exercises and as sources for the problem sections of the text. We also wish to thank Ruth Schowalter and Stephanie Coffin, who provided excellent suggestions that strengthened the text and who assisted with the editing of the materials. Patti Bechi's careful proofreading was invaluable both for her accuracy and attention to detail and for her perceptive and fearless questions about grammar.

We would also like to thank the following ESL professionals who gave comments during the development of this text:

Lida Baker, UCLA
Susan Bangs, Harnsburg Area Community College
John Dumacich, New York University
Jacqueline Milligan, State University of New York at Buffalo
Rebecca Oxford, University of Alabama
Ayse Stromsdorfer, St. Louis University

Graduate students in Patricia Byrd's course on English grammar and pedagogical grammars made many useful observations about explanations and exercises. Most of all, we want to thank the many ESL students who provided writing samples and suggestions that helped us gain a better understanding of the teaching and learning of grammar within the context of written English.

We acknowledge our debt to reference grammars such as Marianne Celce-Murcia and Diane Larsen-Freeman, *The Grammar Book: An ESL/EFL Teacher's Course* and Randolph Quirk, Sidney Greenbaum, Geoffrey Leech, and Jan Svartvik, *A Comprehensive Grammar of the English Language*. Without the work of these grammarians, the writing of teaching grammars would be impossible.

We are especially thankful for the strong support given by the staff at Heinle and Heinle during the writing as well as the publication of this book. David Lee provided thoughtful and realistic guidance in our discussions of ways to make the materials useful and accessible to teachers as well as to students. Anne Sokolsky, Ken Mattsson, and Christine Berryman contributed to the exacting process of editing and publishing a grammar reference book. Stacey Sawyer led us patiently through the maze of activities that change a manuscript into a publication.

Most important has been the unwavering support of Bill Peters, without whose encouragement this book would not have been possible.

Problem-Solution is dedicated to the memory of
Dr. Beverly A. Benson, teacher, administrator,
author, leader, friend.   1943–1993

SECTION

I

Agreement

Noun-Pronoun Agreement

Matching Pronouns and Nouns

Pronouns must match the nouns that they refer to in *number*. This means that singular pronouns are used to refer to singular nouns and that plural pronouns are used to refer to plural nouns. Notice that the pronoun does not agree with the noun that it modifies but with the noun that it refers to. Look at the second example: *our* refers to *my brother and I;* only one car is involved.

The students put **their books** on **their desks.**

My brother and I ride the bus to school because it is difficult to find a place to park **our car.**

The teacher put **her books** on **her desk.**

In English, *he, she,* and *it* reflect the masculine, feminine, or neutral meaning of the noun that each pronoun refers to.

Juan put **his books** on **his desk. He** was pleased when **his teacher** gave **him** an "A" on **his essay.**

Juanita put **her books** on **her desk. She** was pleased when **her teacher** gave **her** an "A" on **her essay.**

While animals are generally referred to as *it*, people who are emotionally close to an animal may refer to it with a masculine or feminine pronoun where appropriate.

```
The dog put its paw in its
trainer's hand.

My dog, Pronto, puts his
paws over his face when he
sleeps.
```

Problems with Pronouns

Problem 1

Not having correct reference for masculine or feminine nouns

Problem	Solution	Revision
*A husband must respect the opinions of her wife.	Many languages do not use separate male and female pronouns. The writer knows that the word *husband* refers to men and *wife* to women but had trouble remembering the correct pronoun form. Change *her* to *his*.	A husband must respect the opinions of his wife.

Problem 2

Not having correct reference for singular or plural nouns

Problem	Solution	Revision
*Each student in this class is required to turn in their research projects at the beginning of the final examination period.	*Each* is singular. The writer has two choices: (1) make the subject plural to agree with the pronoun *their*; (2) change the pronoun and the noun *project* to agree with the singular subject.	All students in this class are required to turn in their research projects at the beginning of the final examination period.

1 **Noun-Pronoun Agreement**

Note that the second choice means that the writer must be careful to avoid using language that would suggest that only men are in the class—unless the class is indeed made up only of male students.

`Each student in this class is required to turn in his/her research project at the beginning of the final examination period.`

`*Many students at this university are unhappy about the high tuition that he must pay.`

The plural noun *students* requires a plural pronoun. The writer has two choices: *they* or *we*. *We* means that the writer is also a student at the school. *They* is ambiguous; it is possible that the writer is not a student.

`Many students at this university are unhappy about the high tuition that they must pay.`

`Many students at this university are unhappy about the high tuition that we must pay.`

Problem 3

Not having correct pronoun reference—inappropriate switching to *you*

Problem	Solution	Revision
☹ `Many people drive too fast even though they know that they can be badly hurt or that you can die in an accident.`	For formal academic writing style, the writer should revise for consistent noun-pronoun reference.	`Many people drive too fast even though they know that they can be badly hurt or that they can die in an accident.`

☹ **A student** must make good use of **your** time.

The writer is making a generalization using a generic noun phrase—*a student*. The pronoun reference needs to be in the formal style. To make the revision, the writer has two choices to avoid using sexist language.

A student must make good use of **his or her** time.

Students must make good use of **their** time.

☛ **Practice 1**

Correct the pronouns, if necessary, in the following sentences.

1. When I first see a person, I often make judgements about their personality.

2. To tell something about a classmate from the way they dress is very difficult because so many students dress in jeans.

3. It is not fair to judge a person by the way they dress.

4. At the end of every quarter, students in my classes have to evaluate their instructors; one question asks whether the instructors identified his or her course goals.

5. I don't think that everyone thinks seriously when they are filling out the evaluation forms.

6. When faculty members see the student evaluation comments, they can adjust their teaching methods and requirements.

7. I wonder if many college students worry about his grades like I do.

8. Every college student should study history and political science because this knowledge will help them become an active member of society and help them make intelligent decisions.

9. If a parent wants her children to turn out right, she must teach or show them her love, support, and compassion.

10. When the relationship between him and his children disintegrates, a parent must use his love to repair the relationship.

☞ Practice 2

Correct the pronouns, if necessary, in the following sentences.

1. Many people have quit smoking recently because they know that smoking can cause health problems; they know that smoking one cigarette can take away ten minutes of your life.

2. Many people know that smoking is bad for their health, but they keep smoking because when you smoke, you can relax more easily.

3. In my opinion, a person cannot be a good parent if you are not caring, concerned, and loving.

4. Most students respect their parents, their teachers, and their friends; if they do not respect these people, they might want to change your behavior.

5. People who are self-employed can use computers for organizing their information base and for processing correspondence.

☞ Practice 3

Correct the pronouns, if necessary, in the following sentences.

1. The world of the 90's is dependent on computers, and the more a person knows about it, the more successful that he can be.

2. Many supermarkets use computers; for example, in some supermarkets, they have installed small computers that can identify where a particular item is kept in the store.

3. To be an educated person, they need to do more than graduate from college.

4. Every person has his/her own personality which affects he/she thinking, feelings, and behavior.

5. A good parent is a parent who can provide love and care to his family members.

Other Units Related to This Topic

✔ **2.** Subject-Verb Agreement

✔ **4.** Avoiding Sexist Language

✔ **9.** Irregular Plural Nouns

✔**10.** Plural and Singular Forms: Consistency of Use in Writing

Subject-Verb Agreement

Technically, grammarians say that all English subjects agree with their verbs when the verbs are present tense forms. That is, in present tense contexts, a plural subject has a simple form of the verb without + *s,* and a singular subject has a verb that adds + *s.* However, writers generally do not have problems except with the omission of + *s* when it is required. Therefore, this section focuses on contexts that require the addition of + *s* to the verb.

Explanation of the Problem

Subject-verb agreement is a relationship between a subject and a verb. The subject requires a particular form for the verb.

Many students are confused because they are not sure which word is the subject. The subjects in these examples are marked with one line and the verbs with two lines.

plural subject with a plural verb

These books seem easy.

singular subject with a singular verb

This book seems easy.

Some students seem to be confused because they associate + *s* with plural nouns. English uses + *s* at the end of most nouns to make the plural form: *book/books.* These students want to make the verb plural, too, by adding + *s.* That change might be logical, but English does not work that way.

plural subject with a plural verb

These books seem easy.

singular subject with a singular verb

This book seems easy.

Strategies for Correct Subject-Verb Agreement

Strategy 1. Learn to find the main subject word. You must know if the main subject word is singular, plural, or noncount. Singular and noncount subjects require changes in the verb. The plural subject uses the simple form of the verb.

Strategy 2. Remember that subject-verb agreement occurs with:
>simple present tense,
>present and past of be (*is/are* and *was/were*),
>present perfect verb forms (*has/have*),
>present and past progressive verb forms, and
>present and past passive verb forms.

Strategy 3. Generally, if the subject has + *s,* then the verb will NOT have + *s.* A plural subject has a simple verb; a singular or noncount subject requires + *s* for the verb. However, a few noncount nouns end in + *s* (*news* and *mathematics*) and take a singular verb, and a few plural nouns are irregular (*children* and *people*) and take a plural verb.

Verbs That Require + *s*

Simple Present Tense. A present tense verb has + *s* when it occurs with a singular count noun or with a noncount noun. Any subject that is not clearly plural is treated as singular.

present tense with singular subject
A student <u>needs</u> a notebook.

present tense with a plural subject
All students <u>need</u> health insurance.

present tense with a noncount noun as subject
Coffee <u>grows</u> especially well in Africa and Latin America.

present tense with a gerund as subject
Buying health insurance <u>is</u> a confusing process for most people.

Be. Subject-verb agreement also occurs with both present and past tense forms of *be*.

present tense of *be*

Because it is very quiet, I am happy to study in the library. My roommate and I are there every afternoon from 3:45 to 5:30.

past tense of *be*

Yesterday, our classroom was very cold. The students were very cold, too.

Progressive and Passive. Because *be* requires subject-verb agreement, progressive and passive verbs change to agree with their subjects.

present progressive

My friends are studying in the library right now.

past progressive

We were still studying when the library closed last night.

present passive

A calculator is required for my math class.

past passive

Our mid-term examination was rescheduled because our teacher was sick. The students were told about the change the morning that we were supposed to take the test.

Present Perfect. Subject-verb agreement also happens with the present perfect verb form.

present perfect

Our teacher has changed the date for the mid-term exam. Some of the students have talked about having a party after the exam.

Subjects That Require Verbs with + *s*

Singular Count Noun. The verb forms listed above change when the subject is a singular noun.

plural noun as main subject word

My friends give a party every weekend.

singular noun as main subject word

My best friend lives in London.

He, It, She. These verbs also change when the subject is *he, she,* or *it.*

plural pronoun as main subject word

They study in the lab.

singular pronoun as main subject word

She studies in the library.

Singular Proper Noun. Singular proper nouns cause the verb to change, too.

singular proper noun as subject

Juan studies at home.

Noncount Noun. Noncount nouns also need subject-verb agreement.

noncount noun as subject

Information about the increased tuition was mailed to all students.

Other Subjects. Generally, any subject that is not clearly plural is treated as singular.

infinitive as subject.

To seek is not to find.

gerund as subject

Studying in the library helps many students to improve their grades.

clause as subject

That he disagrees with our plan is obvious to us all.

Irregular Noun Subjects

Plurals Without + *s*. Writers need to remember that some nouns form their plurals without a change in form: for example, *people* and *police*.

The police <u>are looking</u> for the car thief.

People <u>need</u> to be careful not to <u>leave</u> valuable items in their cars.

Nouns That Have the Same Spelling for Both Singular and Plural. *Series* and *species* use the same spelling for both singular and plural uses. Because they end in *s*, they appear to be plural, but they are sometimes used as singular nouns.

A new series of ESL textbooks <u>is planned</u> for publication next year. The series <u>includes</u> 15 books.

Two series of concerts <u>are presented</u> at the university. One series <u>features</u> jazz music; the second series <u>brings</u> famous rock musicians to campus. Each series <u>includes</u> five concerts.

Nouns That Do Not Have Singular Forms. Some nouns are always plural. These often involve objects that have two parts such as *scissors* and *pants*.

Scissors <u>are</u> a necessary part of everyday life.

Those scissors <u>belong</u> to the department.

These pants <u>do not fit</u> well.

Potential Problems with Certain Subjects

Collective Nouns. *Collective nouns* are words such as *committee, faculty, family, jury,* and *team*. In the United States, these are generally used as singular nouns, treating the group as a whole unit. In other versions of English, speakers treat these nouns as plurals when they think of the members acting as individuals rather than as members of a unit.

singular (*it*)
The committee has made a decision about **its** report to the president.

plural (*they*)
The committee have made a decision about **their** report to the president.

singular (*it*)

The jury is discussing the case. **Its** decision will be announced tomorrow.

plural (*they*)

The jury are discussing the case. **Their** decision will be announced tomorrow.

singular (*it*)

The faculty agrees about the changes in the attendance policy.

plural (*they*)

The faculty disagree about the changes in the attendance policy.

False Plurals. There is a group of nouns that end in *s* that are not plurals. These *false plurals* are words such as *news, mathematics,* and *physics.*

This news from home is really exciting.

Titles. The titles of books, plays, movies, and TV shows are always singular—even if the words in the title are in the plural.

"The Bells" is a famous poem by Edgar Allan Poe. It was published in 1849.

Pair. The word *pair* is singular. Some people are confused when the word is not used. Compare these examples.

This pair of shoes hurts my feet.

These shoes hurt my feet.

Each and **Every.** These words are not problems when they modify a singular noun as in the first example; a singular verb is used. The problem arises for some speakers when *each* or *every* is followed by a plural noun as in the third example. Most educated writers of English use the singular with such subjects; they agree that the actual subject of the sentence is *each* or *every.*

Each book has a table of contents and an index.

Every bicycle should come with a safety helmet.

Each of the books has a table of contents and an index.

Every one of the students has a problem with grammar.

Subject-Verb Agreement

Subject-Verb Agreement with Phrases Used for Counting

A Number of. This phrase is plural.	A number of students <u>are going</u> to Mexico for the summer break to study anthropology.
The Number of. This phrase is singular.	The number of international students at this university <u>has increased</u> by 100% in the past 10 years.
Fractions and Percentages with Plural Nouns. When they modify a plural noun, fractions and percentages take a plural verb.	More than 50% of the students who take calculus <u>fail</u> the course on their first attempt. Half of the students who take calculus <u>fail</u> the course on their first attempt.
Fractions and Percentages with Singular Nouns. When they modify a singular noun, fractions and percentages take a singular verb.	Less than 40% of the book <u>is</u> about current environmental issues. Most of this apple <u>is</u> rotten.
Fractions and Percentages with Noncount Nouns. When they modify a noncount noun, fractions and percentages take a singular verb.	Last spring, <u>75% of Florida's citrus crop</u> <u>was destroyed</u> by the strong winds and rain in the hurricane.
Fractions and Percentages with Collective Nouns. Either a singular or a plural verb can be used when fractions or percentages modify a collective noun.	<u>A third of the team</u> <u>is practicing</u>. Unfortunately, <u>66% of the team</u> <u>are injured</u>.

Subject-Verb Agreement

Subjects That Lead to Difficult Choices

When the subject of a sentence is one of the words in this table, educated native speakers of U.S. English do not agree on the correct form of the verb. In a grammar or composition course, you might ask your teacher for her/his preference. Often the best strategy is to rewrite the sentence to avoid putting one of these forms in the subject position.

None. Some teachers say that *none* is always singular because it means "not one." However, educated native speakers of English do not consistently follow this rule. If *none* modifies a plural noun, the tendency is to use a plural verb. If *none* modifies a noncount noun, the tendency is to use a singular verb. Perhaps a good strategy would be to use another word as in the last two examples.

traditional

None of the books has an index.

None of the books have an index.

None of the coffee tastes good.

avoidance

These books do not have indexes.

***Majority* and *Minority*.** Educated writers of English seem to switch from singular to plural when using these words, depending on different meanings given to the words. The examples show three possible variations. Revision to move the word out of the subject position might be a useful strategy.

Majority/minority in statements about principles for counting and/or voting—use singular verbs.

The minority is not often powerful where the majority rules.

Majority/minority as collective nouns—in the U.S., generally use singular verbs, but the plural form is possible.

In the election, the majority was for a new tax policy.

In the election, the majority were for a new tax policy.

When a plural noun phrase is modified, educated writers seem to prefer the plural verb.

The majority of the students agree on the change.

The minority of the voters were against the tax change.

Subject-Verb Agreement

avoidance by rewording
Minority groups are not often powerful where majority groups rule.

Either . . . or and ***Neither . . . nor.*** The difficulty here results from the form of the second noun. Generally, the noun closest to the verb controls the verb form. A problem is caused if the writer wants to use the pronoun *I*.

Either the teacher or the reference books are wrong.

Either the reference books or the teacher is wrong.

Neither the teacher nor the reference books are wrong.

Neither the reference books nor the teacher is wrong.

Either John or they are in error about the test date.

Either you or I are going to have to go to the bookstore after class.

Either of and ***Neither of.*** The traditional rule says to use a singular form of the verb.

Neither of the answers is correct.

Either of the courses seems useful.

One of. In the first example, the subject of the sentence is singular, so the verb needs + *s*. Problems are caused for some writers because the word closest to the verb is plural. In the third example, a relative clause is connected to the phrase *one of those people*. What is the subject of the relative clause—*one* or *people*? The traditional answer is that the subject of the relative clause is the word *people*. Therefore, the verb agrees with the plural noun *people*. Some writers would avoid the problem by rephrasing the sentence.

problem
*One of my history teachers come from France.

revision
One of my history teachers comes from France.

Our teacher is one of those people who inspire their students to outstanding efforts.

avoidance by rewording
Our teacher inspires her students to make outstanding efforts in her classes.

Problem 1

Using the wrong verb with a singular subject

Problem	Solution	Revision
*My teacher usually call on me first in class; I don't know why.	This sentence shows the basic form of subject-verb agreement. The subject is a singular count noun. The verb is simple present tense. Add + *s* to the verb.	My teacher usually calls on me first in class; I don't know why.
*I really like our biology textbook. It classify the important points and give clear definitions.	The subject is the singular pronoun *it*. Add + *s* to both of the verbs.	I really like our biology textbook. It classifies the important points and gives clear definitions.

Problem 2

Using the wrong verb with a compound subject

Problem	Solution	Revision
*The students and the teacher works in the lab every afternoon.	A compound subject is plural. Remove the + *s* from the verb.	The students and the teacher work in the lab every afternoon.

Problem 3

Using the wrong verb when the subject is a noncount noun that names a field of study

Problem	Solution	Revision
*Chemistry require hours of study.	A noncount noun is used as subject. Add + *s* to a present tense verb.	Chemistry requires hours of study.

*Physics require hours of study.	A noncount noun is used as subject. Add + *s* to a present tense verb. Be careful of noncount nouns that end with + *s;* they are not plural.	Physics requires hours of study.

Problem 4

Using the wrong verb when the subject is a noncount noun

Problem	Solution	Revision
*The information in these articles seem useful for my research paper.	The subject is *information,* a noncount noun. Add + *s* to the verb.	The information in these articles seems useful for my research paper.
*These news about my grades make me very happy.	The subject is *news,* a noncount noun. Change *these* to *this.* Add + *s* to the verb.	This news about my grades makes me very happy.

Problem 5

Trying to make a noncount noun into a plural noun

Problem	Solution	Revision
*Many homeworks are required in all of my classes.	*Homework* is the correct form of this noncount noun. Remove + *s* from the noun. Change the verb to *is. Many* is used only with plural nouns. Change to *a lot of.*	A lot of homework is required in all of my classes.
*Good advices about buying a used car were given on the TV show.	*Advice* is the correct form of this noncount noun. Remove + *s* from the noun. Change the verb to *was.*	Good advice about buying a used car was given on the TV show.

2 **Subject-Verb Agreement**

Problem 6

Using the wrong verb when the subject is separated from the verb by a clause or phrase

Problem	Solution	Revision
*<u>The books</u> that are required for this class <u>costs</u> $65.	The subject is a plural noun—*books*. Remove + *s* from the verb *costs*.	<u>The books</u> that are required for this class <u>cost</u> $65.
*<u>Students</u> at this university <u>has to pay</u> tuition on the same day that they register.	The subject is plural, so use *have*.	<u>Students</u> at this university <u>have to pay</u> tuition on the same day that they register.

Problem 7

Using the wrong verb in a subordinate clause

Problem	Solution	Revision
*Academic advisers provide advice for students <u>who</u> <u>asks</u> for help about their courses.	*Who* means "students." The clause means <u>students</u> ask for advice about their classes.	Academic advisers provide advice for students <u>who</u> <u>ask</u> for help about their courses.
*<u>Statistics courses</u> are required for many different majors because <u>it</u> <u>teaches</u> a method for predicting the future.	The sentence has two problems. (1) The pronoun in the clause must refer to the main subject. Change *it* to *they*. (2) Then, change the verb to match the new subject *they*. Remove + *s* from the verb.	<u>Statistics courses</u> are required for many different majors because <u>they</u> <u>teach</u> a method for predicting the future.

Problem 8

Not selecting the correct form: *there is* or *there are*

Problem	Solution	Correction
*There <u>is</u> no important disadvantages to studying in the library.	*There* does not control the verb. The real "subject" of the sentence is the plural noun *disadvantages*.	There <u>are</u> no important disadvantages to studying in the library.

☞ Practice 1

Draw a line under the word that is the main subject of each clause and two lines under each verb. Then, write the correct form for each verb. There may be more than one mistake in each sentence. The first sentence has been marked, but the problems have not been corrected.

1. There are many different categories of students: those who go to college to learn, those who go to college to socialize, and those who wants to get away from home and be independent.

2. One group of students are the group that work for the grade of "A."

3. A good student give the best of himself; he does every assignment and turn in all assignments on time.

4. When students do their homework, they can participate in class, and they can concentrate more in class than other students who does not prepare for class.

5. An excellent student is one who show interest out of class too.

6. Because he cares about learning, he works hard in order to learn something new, and he also do homework every night.

7. One characteristic of negative students are that they usually do not pay attention to lectures and usually do not turn in assignments on time.

8. Sometimes these students have many absences and does not really care about what they learn in school.

9. Some students rarely do homework because their teacher never grade the homework assignments.

10. The most common and numerous students in many colleges are the "C" students.

☞ Practice 2

Draw a line under the word that is the main subject of each clause and two lines under each verb. Then, write the correct form for each verb. There may be more than one mistake in each sentence; one of the sentences is correct. The first sentence has been marked, but the problems have not been corrected.

1. The university <u>system</u> in the United States <u><u>are</u></u> very different from the university systems in other countries.

2. This college has a small campus that consist of a few small buildings.

3. Usually the first class begin at eight o'clock, and the last class end at ten o'clock.

4. At many colleges, every foreign student have to pass an ESL placement test before taking academic courses.

5. Some ESL students take only ESL classes, and studying in an ESL institute sometimes reduce the chances of hearing American English and making American friends.

6. Taking several classes help to make the time go much faster.

7. Every student who plan to get a degree in nursing and dental hygiene need to pass a state examination.

8. The Regents' Test consist of writing an essay; the essay have to be written in formal English.

9. All students who is taking calculus must pass the departmental final; their homework and their class participation does not count in the grade.

10. One reason why students like taking three classes is that they can qualify for financial aid.

Other Units Related to This Topic

Subject-Verb Agreement

SECTION

II

Articles, Nouns, and Pronouns

UNIT 3

A and *An*

Using *A* or *An*

A and *an* have exactly the same meaning. *An* is used before words that begin with vowel sounds. *A* is used before all other words.

```
I bought an apple.

I bought a book.
```

Using *A* or *An* with Words Beginning with the Letter *H*

Words that begin with the letter *h* can be confusing. If the *h* is pronounced, then the word begins with a consonant sound, and *a* is used. Generally, the *h* is pronounced, so the article *a* is usually required.

happy, history, historical, historic, hot, hypothesis, hysterical

hysterical begins with a consonant sound

```
We saw a
hysterically funny
movie last night.
```

If the *h* is not pronounced, then the word begins with a vowel, and *an* is used.

honest, honor, honorable

honest begins with a vowel sound

```
He seems to be an
honest person.
```

Some people use *an* with the various forms of the word *history*. However, general usage in both the United States and in the United Kingdom is *a* because the *h* is pronounced.

History begins with a consonant sound.

`I bought` **`a history book`** `to`
`learn more about Mexico.`

A few people prefer this usage although *historic* begins with a consonant sound.

`The President's visit to`
`our city was` **`an historic`**
`moment.`

Using *A* or *An* with Words Beginning with the Letter *E*

The letter *e* usually represents a vowel sound, so *an* is usually the correct choice with such words.

`an eagle, an elegant dress`

However, in some words the letters *eu* are pronounced like *you*. These words need *a*.

`a Eurodollar, a European, a`
`Eurasian`

Using *A* or *An* with Words Beginning with the Letter *U*

Usually the letter *u* represents a vowel sound, so *an* is the correct choice.

ugly, ulcer, umbrella, umpire, uncle

`I bought` **`an`**
`umbrella` `at the`
`sale at the`
`bookstore.`

The prefix *ultra-* begins with a vowel sound. Therefore, compound phrases such as the following are preceded by *an: ultra fast, ultra modern, ultrasonic, ultrasound,* and *ultraviolet.* Check your dictionary to find out if the phrase is written as two words or as one word.

`A doctor can use`
`an ultrasound`
`machine` `to check`
`the health of an`
`unborn baby.`

3 *A and An*

The prefix *un-* begins with a vowel sound. Therefore, words such as the following are preceded by *an: unconscious, unhappy, unknown,* and *unusual.*

```
He made an unusual
request.
```

The prefix *under-* begins with a vowel sound. Therefore, compound phrases such as the following are preceded by *an: underachiever, underage, undercover, underestimate,* and *underground.*

```
I park my car in
an underground
garage.
```

However, *u* is sometimes pronounced like *you,* so *a* is the correct choice because the word actually begins with a consonant sound.

union, unique, unit, unitary, universal, and *universe*

```
She prefers going
to a university
rather than a
college.
```

Also, adjectives and nouns that are formed with the prefix *uni-* have this pronunciation and so use *a: unicorn, unicycle, unification, uniform, unilateral, unilinear,* and *unilingual.*

```
The project
requires a uniform
effort by all the
students.
```

Meaning of *A* and *An*

Indefinite Meaning. *A* and *an* are used with singular count nouns for indefinite meaning. The first reference to this particular professor is with *a* because the writer thinks that the reader does not share knowledge with him/her. The second mention of the professor uses *the* because the writer and the reader now have the same information.

```
I met a professor from
Japan at the reception for
new students. Her daughter
is in my ESL class. I saw
the professor again later
at the concert of
traditional Chinese music.
```

A and *An*

Generic Meaning. *A* and *an* are also used with singular count nouns for generic meaning. *A doctor* and *a lawyer* refer to professions rather than to people. The second reference does NOT change to *the* because the meaning is still about the name of a profession.

My sister is **a doctor.** As **a doctor,** she must work long hours to help her patients.

A lawyer must explain the laws clearly and accurately. **A lawyer** must, therefore, be trained in the skillful use of language.

Problems with *A* and *An*

Problem 1

Using *an* before words that begin with a consonant sound

Problem	Solution	Revision
*Once you try a cigarette and enjoy smoking it, you are addicted to smoking, and you will do it as **an habit.**	The word *habit* begins with a consonant sound, so substitute *a* for *an.*	Once you try a cigarette and enjoy smoking it, you are addicted to smoking, and you will do it as **a habit.**
*Here in the U.S., I feel freer and happier because no one will call me "Yankee," **an child** of mixed white and Asian heritage.	The word *child* begins with a consonant sound, so substitute *a* for *an.*	Here in the U.S., I feel freer and happier because no one will call me "Yankee," **a child** of mixed white and Asian heritage.

Problem 2

Using *a* before words that begin with a vowel sound

Problem	Solution	Revision
*Of course, I am not **a exception.**	*Exception* begins with a vowel sound, so use *an.*	Of course, I am not **an exception.**

A and An

*Without evaluations, administrators would not know how well **a instructor** teaches.	*Instructor* begins with a vowel sound, so use *an*.	Without evaluations, administrators would not know how well **an instructor** teaches.
*I want to be **a honest person**.	*Honest* begins with a vowel sound, so use *an*.	I want to be **an honest person**.

Problem 3

Using *a* or *an* with noncount nouns

Problem	Solution	Revision
*My parents did not give me **a permission** to study here until I passed the TOEFL.	*Permission* is a noncount noun. Do not use an article for this meaning. Remove *a*.	My parents did not give me **permission** to study here until I passed the TOEFL.
*It is important to have **a fun** during a vacation.	*Fun* is a noncount noun. Remove *a*.	It is important to have **fun** during a vacation.

Problem 4

Dividing *an* from *other* in the word *another*.

Problem	Solution	Revision
*I think I should learn more about my native language before I learn **an other** one.	*Another* is written as one word. Look up the pronunciation for the word in your dictionary. Notice that the pronunciation divides the words between *a/nother*.	I think I should learn more about my native language before I learn **another** one.

A and An

Leaving out *a* or *an* with a singular count noun

Problem	Solution	Revision
*She needs **calculator** for her physics class.	A singular count noun must have an article or a determiner. This example needs *a* for generic meaning.	She needs **a calculator** for her physics class.

Using *a* or *an* with a plural noun

Problem	Solution	Revision
*Course evaluations are very important to **a administrators,** faculty, and students.	*Administrators* is a plural noun used for generic meaning. No article should be used. Remove *a*.	Course evaluations are very important to **administrators,** faculty, and students.
*Secondly, throughout history, war has been used to stop the invasion of **an independent countries.**	The writer is making a generalization. Generic meaning can be given with a singular noun or with a plural noun. The singular form is *a/an* + noun. The plural form does not use an article. See Unit 8, "Generic Meaning" for more information.	Secondly, throughout history, war has been used to stop the invasion of **an independent country.** Secondly, throughout history, war has been used to stop the invasion of **independent countries.**

3   *A and An*

Problem 7

Using *a* or *an* where *the* is required

Problem	Solution	Revision
*Without this main ingredient, even **a best cook** could not make a delicious meal.	*The* is used with the superlative forms of adjectives.	Without this main ingredient, even **the best cook** could not make a delicious meal.
*They spend their vacation at **a beach, a mountain,** or another vacation place.	The expression used for generalizations about vacation spots uses *the.* English-speakers go to the beach or the mountains for a vacation.	They spend their vacation at **the beach, the mountains,** or another vacation place.

☞ **Practice 1**

As appropriate, add *a* or *an* to each of these words or phrases.

1._____ hundred dollars   5._____ house   9._____ university professor

2._____ angry customer   6._____ big house   10._____ uninsured driver

3._____ hungry child   7._____ ugly house   11._____ eighth of a pound

4._____ unhappy student   8._____ holiday   12._____ great deal of energy

☞ **Practice 2**

Three of these sentences have an unnecessary *a/an*. Place an X over the article that should be removed.

1. The university sent me an information about its biology department.

2. Our math teacher gave us a lot of homework to do over the weekend.

3. Our math teacher gave us a homework to do over the weekend.

4. I try to learn a new vocabulary every day.

5. The university sent me an informative brochure about its biology department.

A and An **3**

☞ Practice 3

Two of these sentences are correct. Three need to have articles added. Decide which sentences need articles and which articles to use.

1. We need information about the final exam.

2. She is unhappy about the cold weather.

3. Jose usually studies in university library.

4. My sister is student at the University of Iowa.

5. I need computer to use to do my homework.

☞ Practice 4

Add or change *a* or *an* in the following sentences. You may need to change more than one article in a sentence.

1. The High Museum of Art has variety of famous paintings from many countries.

2. Downtown Atlanta has underground shopping mall that is called Underground Atlanta.

3. There is an restaurant that has beautiful and relaxing atmosphere for people who visit Underground Atlanta.

4. Stone Mountain is good place for visitors who are interested in camping, hiking, and swimming.

5. Disney World in Florida is a enjoyable place, and it is close to Sea World, MGM Grand, and Universal Studios.

Other Units Related to This Topic

✔ 5. Definite and Indefinite Meaning for Nouns and Articles

✔ 7. Noncount Nouns

✔ 8. Nouns Without Articles

✔11. *The*

3 *A and An*

4

Avoiding Sexist Language

Sexist Language Defined

In the past, masculine forms of the pronoun (*he, his, him, himself*) and the nouns *man* and *mankind* were used to represent all people.

☹ **Man** must learn to live peacefully with other **men** and with all the other forms of life on this earth.

However, many professions, publications, and individual instructors now require that writers avoid that older usage because it ignores the existence of women. Using masculine words to refer to all people is called *sexist language*. The word *parent* includes both fathers and mothers. A more accurate sentence would use a plural pronoun. If the writer is focused on fathers, then *a father* or *fathers* must be used.

☹ **A** good **parent** must take care of **his** children and help them grow up to be responsible citizens.

Good parents must take care of **their** children and help them grow up to be responsible citizens.

A good father must take care of **his** children and help them grow up to be responsible citizens.

Good fathers must take care of **their** children and help them grow up to be responsible citizens.

He, him, his, and *himself* are reserved for masculine subjects. So far, no women have played on the Brazilian soccer team. If that changes, then pronoun use will need to change, too.

When a member of the Brazilian soccer team becames a national hero, **he** is famous in the same ways that basketball, football, and baseball stars are famous in the U.S.

She, her, hers, and *herself* are used for feminine subjects.

The term super woman is used for the professional woman who also has a family. **She** might be a full-time member of a law firm, but **she** is also a full-time wife and mother. Generally, **her** time must be carefully managed, and **she** must have a lot of energy.

This change in usage was originally part of the feminist movement of the late 20th century. However, the usage is broadly accepted in the United States and does not carry the political overtones that it once did. This style is the accepted standard for written communication by the government, in education, and in professions (and their publications).

Since workers at road construction sites now include both men and women, warning signs are being changed. In the past the signs said "Men at Work." Now many signs simply say "Workers" or "Crew at Work."

Strategies for Avoiding Sexist Language

Strategy 1: Use Plural Forms. Where possible, use plural forms of nouns and pronouns. This choice makes your writing easier to manage because you do not have to remember to use one of the combination forms. Also, this style makes it clear that you are writing about all people together rather than just about men or just about women.

problem: not all teachers are men

☹ **A teacher** must work with **his** students to help them learn quickly.

revision

Teachers must work with **their** students to help them learn quickly.

Strategy 2: Combine *She* and *He*.

If the plural is not selected, use a combination pronoun that combines both male and female forms. This combination must be consistently used throughout a particular composition. Select one form, and use it consistently. You have these choices for subject forms: *s/he, she/he,* or *he/she.* For object forms, these choices are available: *him/her* or *her/him.* For possessive form, you can use either *his/her* or *her/his.* You can also substitute *or* for the */* to write *his or her, her or his,* and so forth.

A teacher must work with **her/his** students to help them learn quickly.

A teacher must work with **her or his** students to help them learn quickly.

A teacher must work with **his/her** students to help them learn quickly.

A teacher must work with **his or her** students to help them learn quickly.

Strategy 3: Avoid Certain Words.

When writing about all people, avoid the word *man* and compounds with *man* such as *chairman.* Use *people* and various other words that clearly include both men and women. The following words and phrases should not be used to refer to all people as a group: *man, mankind, man's achievements, the average man, manpower,* and so forth. In addition, universities now generally use either *chairperson* or *chair* rather than *chairman* even when referring to a male.

Through **their** greed and carelessness, **people** have destroyed much of the earth's surface, turning it to desert and destroying other life forms.

The **chairperson** of our department, Dr. James Jones, has **his** doctorate from the University of Nebraska.

The **chair** of our department, Dr. Mary Gill, has just published **her** tenth book.

Strategy 4: Be Clear About Meaning.

If your topic is about either men or women, state your topic early in the composition. For example, if you are writing about fathers, then do not use the word *parent* unless you are writing about fathers and mothers together.

In this essay, I will explore changes in the roles of **the father** that have occurred in the U.S. in the 20th century. **His** responsibilities to **his** wife and to **his** children have gone through great changes.

32   **Avoiding Sexist Language**

Professional Association Guidelines for Publication and Presentations

Avoidance of language that involves sexual bias is now a requirement for professional associations in the United States and many other countries. As an example of the requirement by professions for publication of articles in their journals, these rules are given in the *Publication Manual of the American Psychological Association* (1984, 3rd Edition, pp. 43–45) in its "Guidelines for Nonsexist Language in APA Journals."

The American Psychological Association (1984) made the following statement:

> In 1982, the APA Publications and Communications Board adopted a policy that requires authors who are submitting their manuscripts to an APA journal to use nonsexist language, that is, to avoid in their manuscripts language that could be construed as sexist. (p. 44)

A Note to Upper Division and Graduate Students

The style manual for your major field of study will have a discussion about the language requirements of your profession for publication and for presentation of research at conferences. Generally, the style manual will give the profession's rules and will also illustrate typical problems encountered by writers in that profession. It would be wise for academic writers to be aware of the style manuals used in their fields and to study the approaches adopted by their professions for research and for writing that do not exhibit sexual or ethnic bias.

☛ Practice

Use one of the strategies discussed above to revise the sexist language in the following sentences.

1. Throughout the history of mankind, war has been the main way countries have obtained additional land.

2. If a parent wants his children to grow into responsible adults, he should provide them with discipline, support, and guidance.

3. In my opinion, a person cannot be a good doctor if he is not caring, concerned, and competent.

4. In the Stone Age, cavemen obtained their knowledge by studying the drawings and pictures of previous tribes.

5. Every student has been tested at least once in his life.

6. I would also ask if a professor is biased about his students.

7. A parent must use her love and understanding when she and her child disagree.

8. The chairman of the Recruitment and Retention Committee was ten minutes late to the last meeting.

9. If an employer dresses well, then he presents a positive image to his employees and customers.

10. A student on a student visa is permitted to work on campus, and he is paid $5.25 an hour.

Other Units Related to This Topic

✔ 1. Noun-Pronoun Agreement

✔10. Plural and Singular Forms: Consistency of Use in Writing

Avoiding Sexist Language

5

Definite and Indefinite Meaning for Nouns and Articles

English nouns combine with articles and determiners for three basic meanings: indefinite meaning, definite meaning, and generic meaning. The terminology for articles causes some confusion about meaning: indefinite and definite articles are used for more than indefinite and definite meaning. They are also used for generic meaning.

Combining Articles and Nouns for Generic, Definite, and Indefinite Meaning

Generic Noun Phrases. *Generic* means that the nouns refer to a whole class of people or things. The example is a generalization about categories of things and people. It is not about a particular worker in a particular factory but about all workers in all types of automobile factories.

```
Computers have changed the
skills needed by a worker
in the automobile industry.
```

Definite Noun Phrases. *Definite* means that the writer thinks that the listener knows what is being talked about. We write *the sun* or *the earth* because we all share this same meaning.

```
The earth is one of nine
planets that circle around
the sun.
```

35

Indefinite Noun Phrases. Indefinite noun phrases are used to introduce new information. *Indefinite* means that the writer thinks that the reader does NOT know what is being talked about. This example uses the beginning of a folk story to show how indefinite articles are used to introduce new information. After the information has been introduced, *the* replaces *a: a miller* becomes *the miller; a river* becomes *the river; a job* becomes *the job.*

Once **a miller** lived near **a river** with his wife and his daughter. When **the river** dried up, **the miller** could no longer grind grain, so he took **a job** digging ditches. **The job** paid very little, and **the miller** and his family were very hungry. . . .

Changing from Indefinite to Definite Meaning

Often a writer starts with indefinite meaning and then changes to definite meaning because the noun has been identified. The writer assumes that meaning is now shared with the reader. Definite meaning is often indicated by using pronouns such as *he, she,* and *it.* Definite meaning can also be indicated by using words such as *this, that, these,* and *those. The* can also be used for definite meaning. When *the* is used, this change to definite meaning is called *second reference.*

I met **a student** from Iceland at the reception. **She** is studying economics here.

They bought **some eggs** and **some oranges. The eggs** are in the refrigerator. They ate **the oranges** for breakfast.

Using *The* for Definite Meaning

In the following situations, you can expect to use *the* with nouns for definite meaning.

1. Unique. The noun refers to something that is unique for everyone in the world.

the sun, the moon

2. Setting. The noun is made specific by its setting. Everyone in the classroom will understand the same meaning for these nouns.

the blackboard, the students

3. Parts of a Whole. The nouns refer to the parts of some whole that is being talked about.

In my apartment **the floors** are covered with carpet except in **the kitchen.**

4. Second Reference. A writer can mention something one time using *a* or *an* because the reader does not share the same information. After that first use, the writer changes to *the* because the information is shared with the reader.

I borrowed **some butter, an egg,** and **an apple** from a neighbor. I ate **the apple. The butter** and **the egg** are in the refrigerator.

5. Phrases/Clauses. A writer can make a noun definite by adding a defining phrase or clause.

We met **the president of our university** at the reception for new students.

6. Superlatives/Numbers. Because parts of sets are considered to have shared and definite meaning, *the* is used for phrases, such as *the tallest student, the second teacher,* and *the last answer* on *the test.*

He is **the fastest runner** on our team. He is always **the first person** to finish a race.

7. Known to a Particular Group. Members of a particular group share meanings. If you say "the prime minister," people in Canada will assume that you mean their prime minister.

The prime minister went to Japan yesterday.

8. Pointing. A speaker can point (with a finger, a nod of the head) at something and use *the* because s/he assumes that the listener then understands the particular object being talked about. This use is almost impossible for a writer.

She pointed at the table and said, "Please hand me **the calculator** over there."

Definite and Indefinite Meaning/Nouns and Articles

☞ Practice 1

Add *the,* where necessary, to the following sentences. Some sentences need more than one change, and some sentences are correct.

1. Homework is an essential part of many college courses.

2. I finished homework for my writing class in only two hours.

3. Students who are in my writing class have become my close friends.

4. Students are often very busy with family, work, and school obligations.

5. Advice is sometimes difficult to follow even when advice makes sense.

6. Advice that my counselor gave me last year was best advice that I have ever received.

7. English language has many exceptions to its rules.

8. Many foreign students think that English is a difficult language to learn.

9. Computers have become necessary in many people's lives.

10. Computers in writing lab at my university are IBM compatible.

☞ Practice 2

Add *the* to the following sentences, where needed.

The Size of the United States

[1]Before coming to United States, I had no idea of size of this country. [2]After looking at a map, I could see that United States occupies nearly half of North America. [3]And besides China and Canada, United States is considered one of biggest countries in the world. [4]However, this information came from a book. [5]I didn't realize size of this country until I came here. [6]My flight from Seattle to Miami took almost five hours. [7]In other words, traveling across United States in a 747 jet takes almost five hours. [8]Besides, when I looked down from plane, I could see highways that seemed unending. [9]One day, I felt hungry; unfortunately, there was nothing in my refrigerator. [10]I had to drive for fifteen minutes to find a place to get some food. [11]Size of this country is hard to describe to someone who has never been here.

☞ Practice 3

Add *the* to the following sentences, where needed.

Reasons I Enjoy This Class

[1]There are several reasons why my ESL class is most enjoyable class for me this semester. [2]To begin with, it is my first class of day. [3]Because it starts at

10:00 AM, I can sleep late and still arrive in classroom on time. [4]Furthermore, teacher is very good, and her attitude makes ESL writing class more enjoyable. [5]Teacher is also a nice person who cares about her students and who gives us handouts and uses blackboard very well. [6]She teaches us how to write better and how to prepare for exams. [7]English is not an easy language to learn, but it is an important language for business. [8]To be a successful businessman, I know that I need to concentrate on learning English language while I am in United States. [9]In conclusion, time, teacher, and importance of language make my ESL class enjoyable to me.

☞ Practice 4

Add *the* to the following sentences, where needed.

My Most Prized Possession

[1]Most prized possession that I own is a piece of jewelry that is called a "janjar." [2]This piece of jewelry is important to me because it has been in my family a long time and it is very valuable. [3]Janjar that I have was given to me by my grandmother at my wedding, and it was given to her by her mother at her wedding. [4]I will cherish it for rest of my life and then give it to my daughter if I have one in future. [5]It is oldest piece of jewelry in my family, and it is always given to oldest daughter in family. [6]I value it because out of ten grandchildren I was oldest grandaughter. [7]Janjar is also worth about $7,500 now, but when my grandmother got it from her mother, it was worth only about $75. [8]These are reasons why I value my most prized possession.

Other Units Related to This Topic

✔ **3.** *A* and *An*

✔ **6.** Generic Meaning for Nouns and Articles

✔ **7.** Noncount Nouns

✔ **8.** Nouns Without Articles

✔**11.** *The*

Definite and Indefinite Meaning/Nouns and Articles 39

Generic Meaning for Nouns and Articles

We often communicate about groups of people or classes of things rather than about particular objects or people. We communicate about the kind of thing rather than the particular object. All of the articles are used for various generic meanings.

Combining Articles and Nouns for Generic Meaning

These examples illustrate the *generic* meaning of nouns. Notice that all types of nouns (singular, plural, noncount) and all articles can be used for generic meaning.

plural generic
Teachers give **tests.**

singular generic
The elephant can be found in Africa and India.

singular generic
He is **a teacher.**

noncount generic
Water is necessary for all forms of **life.**

Plural Nouns in Generalizations

Plural nouns without articles can be used to refer to classes or groups.

Students take **tests.**

Lions live in Africa.

Computers are used for word processing.

The + Singular Noun in Generalizations

The with a singular noun is often used for generic meaning. This generic type is the one preferred in technical or informative writing on plants, animals, inventions, and other technical topics.

The alligator lives throughout Florida.

The telephone has changed human communication.

A or *An* + Singular Noun in Generalizations

A with a singular noun is used to refer to one member or one example of a type. The meaning is about general types and not about particular instances. It means something like "one of this kind of thing."

I want to be **an engineer.**

He wants to buy **a computer.**

A computer has three major components.

Noncount Nouns in Generalizations

For generic meaning, noncount nouns do not have articles.

Music is found in all human cultures.

I really enjoy listening to **music** on the radio.

☞ Practice 1

Write a generalization using each of the following nouns.

1. coffee _____

2. water _____

3. computers _____

4. a computer _____

5. students _____

6. a student _____

7. the radio _____

8. radios _____

9. a radio _____

☞ Practice 2

Select two important concepts from your field of study. Write a generalization about each concept.

Concept #1: _____

Concept #2: _____

☞ Practice 3

Circle the generic nouns in the following sentences.

Students and Tests

[1] Students take many tests during their years at school. [2] These tests may be objective or subjective. [3] A conscientious student learns how to study for tests and how to take tests effectively. [4] Counselors often conduct seminars to help students study for tests. [5] The seminar that I took yesterday was very good, and I hope it helps everyone do better on our mid-term tests. [6] Advice is always useful.

Edgar Allan Poe

[1] Edgar Allan Poe, born in Boston in 1809, is still famous as a poet and a short story writer. [2] His short story "The Murders in the Rue Morgue" is credited as being the first example of detective fiction. [3] His most popular stories include "The Fall of the House of Usher," "The Gold Bug," and "The Cask of Amontillado." [4] His best known poems are "The Raven," "Ulalume," and "Annabel Lee."

Water

[1] Water is a chemical compound of hydrogen and oxygen. [2] Occurring almost everywhere in nature, it takes the form of ice, snow, water, and steam. [3] Snow, which is frozen water vapor in the form of ice crystals, is the purest natural form of water. [4] These crystals form in clouds at temperatures below freezing.

Used Cars

[1] Every year Americans spend more than $54 billion to buy more than 17 million used cars. [2] The Federal Trade Commission's Used Car Rule requires used car dealers to place large stickers, called "Buyers Guides," in the left front windows of used vehicles that they offer for sale.

Tigers

[1] Tigers are the largest member of the cat family. [2] Found in Asia, tigers can be divided into several geographic subgroups. [3] While tigers usually eat wild animals, old or wounded tigers may attack human beings. [4] Tigers are, however, no match for elephants.

Other Units Related to This Topic

6 **Generic Meaning for Nouns and Articles**

Noncount Noun Defined

Noncount nouns are words like *information, mathematics, sugar,* and *water.* Noncount nouns do not have a singular or a plural. For subject-verb agreement, noncount nouns use the same verb form as singular nouns.

The teacher gave us **information** about the test.

Mathematics has always been easy for me.

Sugar remains Cuba's major agricultural product.

Articles and Noncount Nouns

A and *an* cannot be used with noncount nouns.

*I need **an information** about this school.

I need **information** about this school.

I need **some information** about this school.

In generalizations, noncount nouns are used without an article.

generic meaning for some noncount nouns for natural phenomena

We will have terrible weather this weekend. We expect **rain, thunder, lightning, sleet,** and **snow.**

generic meaning for the noncount noun *furniture*

```
That store rents furniture
to students.
```

The and other determiners can be used for definite meaning.

definite meaning for a noncount noun

```
The furniture that I rented
with my roommates is cheap
but durable.
```

definite meaning for a noncount noun

```
I rented my furniture from
a store near my apartment.
```

Noncount Nouns That End with *S*

Here is a list of noncount nouns that end with the letter *s*. These words look like plural nouns, but they are noncount nouns. *AIDS, arthritis, civics, diabetes, economics, laryngitis, mathematics, measles, mumps, news, physics, politics, tennis, tuberculosis*

Using the Names of Diseases and Medical Conditions

When writing generalizations about a disease or condition, use the noncount noun without an article.

```
Measles can be a dangerous
disease.
```

When referring to a particular instance of a disease or condition, some words can use *the* while others do not use an article.

```
I had the measles when I
was six years old.

John's mother has diabetes.
```

An Alphabetized List of Common Noncount Nouns

The following list provides a sample of words that are usually used as noncount nouns. It is not a complete list. Remember that for certain meanings, some of these words have count forms.

advertising	chocolate	garbage	lead	penicillin	spinach
advice	civics	gas	leisure	pepper[1]	steel
AIDS	cloth	gasoline	lemonade	Pepsi	stroke
air	clothing	glass	lettuce	permission	sugar
anger	coal	gold	lightning	petroleum	swimming
applause	coffee	grass	love	photography	tea
asthma	coke	gravel	luck	physics	tear gas
astronomy	concrete	gravity	luggage	plastic	tennis
bacon	confidence	gravy	lumber	poetry	wealth
baggage	copper	hail	machinery	polio	weather
barley	corn	hair	mail	politics	wheat
baseball	cornmeal	ham	mathematics	sand	wine
basketball	cotton	happiness	measles	sanity	wood
beauty	courage	hatred	meat	satisfaction	wool
beef	cream	health	melancholy	scenery	work
beer	crime	helium	music	selfishness	yogurt
behavior	curiosity	help	neon	serenity	
biology	darkness	helpfulness	news	silver	
birth control	dew	jogging	nitrous oxide	slang	
blood	diabetes	juice	oatmeal	sleet	
bookkeeping	dirt	justice	oil	smallpox	
bowling	fog	kerosene	oxygen	smoke	
brass	food	knowledge	paper	snow	
bread	football	lamb	pasta	soap	[1]black,
checkers	fruit	laryngitis	patriotism	soccer	ground, or
cheese	fun	laughter	pay	soup	red but not
chicken	furniture	laziness	peace	spaghetti	bell or green

Identifying Noncount Nouns

1. Things that Come in Small Pieces   *barley, cornmeal, flour, grass, gravel, oatmeal, pepper (black, ground, or white), popcorn, rice, salt, sand, sugar, wheat*

2. Wholes Made Up of Similar Parts (the parts are often count nouns)	*baggage, cash, clothing, equipment, food, fruit, furniture, jewelry, luggage, lumber, machinery, mail, merchandise, money*
3. Subjects of Study	*astronomy, biology, bookkeeping, civics, economics, English, ESL, Chinese, computer science, economics, engineering, geology, German, history, mathematics, physics, political science*
4. Abstractions	*advice, anger, beauty, curiosity, enjoyment, equality, fun, happiness, hatred, help, helpfulness, ignorance, importance, information, justice, knowledge, laziness, love, luck, patriotism, peace, relaxation, sanity, serenity, selfishness, trouble, work*
5. Liquids and Fluids	*blood, coffee, gasoline (gas), juice, kerosene, lemonade, milk, oil, tea, water, wine*
6. Gases	*air, carbon dioxide, carbon monoxide, ether, helium, hydrogen, neon, nitrous oxide, oxygen, smoke, sodium pentothal, tear gas*
7. Solids and Minerals	*brass, concrete, copper, cotton, glass, gold, ice, iron, lead, mercury, silver, steel, wood*
8. Sports and Types of Recreation (many are formed with *+ing*)	*baseball, basketball, bowling, bridge, checkers, chess, football, hockey, jogging, soccer, swimming, tennis, volleyball*

9. Natural Phenomena	*dew, fog, gravity, hail, humidity, ice, lightning, mist, rain, sleet, snow, thunder*
10. Diseases/Medical Procedures	*AIDS, asthma, birth control, cancer, diabetes, emphysema, flu, laryngitis, measles, mumps, muscular dystrophy, polio, smallpox, stroke, tuberculosis*

Problems with Noncount Nouns

Problem 1

The following nouns are often used by students in academic writing. A noncount noun does not have a plural form. Remember that for generic meaning, noncount nouns cannot have an article.

Problem	Solution	Revision
*My teacher gives us **the homeworks** every night.	*Homework* is a noncount noun. Remove +s. Remove *the*.	My teacher gives us **homework** every night.
*I need **informations** about your university.	*Information* is a noncount noun. Remove +s.	I need **information** about your university.
*In this class, students gain **knowledges** about world history.	*Knowledge* is a noncount noun. Remove +s.	In this class, students gain **knowledge** about world history.
*Our teacher promised to help us learn new **vocabularies** in this class.	*Vocabulary* is a noncount noun. Remove +ies.	Our teacher promised to help us learn new **vocabulary** in this class.

Noncount Nouns

Using articles with noncount nouns for generic meaning

Problem	Solution	Revision
*I will ask for **an advice** from my close friends and my family.	*A* and *an* cannot be used with noncount nouns. Remove *a*. The writer has other choices that are shown in the revisions.	I will ask for **advice** from my close friends and my family. I will ask for **some advice** from my close friends and my family. I will ask for **a lot of advice** from my close friends and my family.

Problem 3

Not using the correct verb for subject-verb agreement when a noncount noun is the subject

Problem	Solution	Revision
***Mathematics** are really interesting to me.	*Mathematics* looks like a plural noun, but it is not. Change the verb to *is*.	**Mathematics** is really interesting to me.

☞ Practice 1

Place a check by each noncount noun in the following list.

1. _____ idea
2. _____ coffee
3. _____ school
4. _____ homework
5. _____ news
6. _____ mathematics

7. _____ salary
8. _____ advice
9. _____ money
10. _____ information
11. _____ dollar
12. _____ list (*continued*)

Noncount Nouns

13. _____ tuition	22. _____ course
14. _____ suggestion	23. _____ clothing
15. _____ emotion	24. _____ vocabulary
16. _____ government	25. _____ assignment
17. _____ cash	26. _____ equipment
18. _____ shirt	27. _____ calculator
19. _____ honesty	28. _____ politics
20. _____ computer	29. _____ coin
21. _____ education	30. _____ laboratory

☞ **Practice 2**

Correct any errors with the noncount nouns in the following sentences.

1. Most companies store their informations in computers, and students need to learn how to use these computers before they graduate from college.

2. I like to study and would like to get more knowledges from books, but I have a limited amount of money for my education.

3. My friends gave me many advices about how to study better and how to improve my English.

4. Students can learn some new vocabularies through reading books and through conversations with native speakers.

5. People like to visit San Francisco because of its cable cars, Golden Gate Bridge, and good transportations.

Other Units Related to This Topic

✔ **2.** Subject-Verb Agreement

✔ **3.** *A* and *An*

✔ **5.** Definite and Indefinite Meaning for Nouns and Articles

✔ **6.** Generic Meaning for Nouns and Articles

✔ **8.** Nouns Without Articles

✔**11.** *The*

Noncount Nouns

Nouns Without Articles

Contexts Where Articles Are Not Used

Noncount nouns cannot have articles for generic meaning.	**Water** is necessary for **life**.
Plural nouns cannot have articles for generic meaning.	**Doctors** study for many years.
	Children need love and direction from **adults**.

Contexts Where Articles Must Be Used

A singular count noun must have an article or a determiner for each of its possible meanings.

generic meaning
Their father is **a doctor**.

indefinite meaning
I met **a doctor** at the reception. His office is near my home.

definite meaning
I bought **this car** from **the friend** that you met at **the party**.

Noncount nouns need articles or determiners to show definite meaning.	**The water in this city** is badly polluted.
Plural nouns need articles or determiners to show definite meaning.	definite meaning **The teachers** at **this university** spend a lot of time talking with students outside of class. definite meaning **These books** are required for my ESL classes.
The is required with a singular noun for one of the generic choices. The first sentence is about all doctors.	generic meaning **The doctor** studies for many years. generic meaning **The telephone** and **the computer** have changed human communication.

Problems with Articles

Problem 1

Using *the* incorrectly for generic meaning

Problem	Solution	Revision
*Today, even **the supermarkets** use computers for many different purposes.	The writer means all supermarkets, not a particular group of supermarkets. For this generic meaning, the writer has two choices: (1) *supermarkets* or (2) *the supermarket.*	Today, even **supermarkets** use computers for many different purposes. Today, even **the supermarket** uses computers for many different purposes.

Nouns Without Articles

*The smoking in public causes harm to others.	Smoking is a gerund used as a noncount noun. It refers to this type of activity rather than to any particular action. Remove the.	Smoking in public causes harm to others.

Leaving out *the* when it is needed for definite meaning

Problem	Solution	Revision
*At this university, students need knowledge of computers to use **library's computerized catalog** or to go to **computer lab** to do class projects.	The writer is referring to a particular library and to a particular computer lab. This is definite meaning. Add *the*.	At this university, students need knowledge of computers to use **the library's computerized catalog** or to go to **the computer lab** to do class projects.

☞ **Practice 1**

Choose the correct form below: with or without an article.

1. I enjoy television/the television.

2. Two of my main problems are money/the money and transportation/the transportation.

3. School/The school that I attend is very expensive.

4. Soccer/The soccer is my favorite sport, but I also enjoy tennis/the tennis.

5. Life/The life would be very lonely without friends/the friends.

6. My roommate wrote her research paper about work/the work of Sister Teresa.

7. Some students ignore homework/the homework.

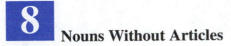

8 **Nouns Without Articles** 53

8. After classes/the classes are over, I usually go to the library with friends/the friends.

9. Calculators/The calculators are required for Math 117.

10. After graduating from college/the college, I plan to travel for six months.

☛ Practice 2

Underline the 16 count nouns in the following paragraph. Then, add an article (*a, an, the*) to the six singular count nouns. (*Television* is being used as a noncount noun; the other noncount nouns in the paragraph below are _____, _____, and _____.)

Television as Education

[1]Television is educational, enlightening instrument. [2]By just sitting in front of television set, we can travel to exotic, wonderful places and watch programs that discuss different countries. [3]In addition to local news, television brings us information about other countries. [4]Television also brings information about educational programs, college courses, scientific experiments, and medical research. [5]We also get current news from all over world; this news helps us visualize many different world events from natural disasters to revolutions. [6]Finally, at the end of stressful day, we can relax while watching funny show or classical music program.

☛ Practice 3

Add either an article (*a, an, the*) or +*s* to the 27 count nouns in the following paragraph. The verb will often help you decide whether the subject should be singular (an article) or plural (+*s*).

Modern Disasters

[1]In modern times, disaster have become increasing threat. [2]Many of these disaster include accident that are caused by technological accident. [3]Such incident include fire, explosion, release of toxic substance, transportation accident, dam failure, and many other mishap. [4]The toxic chemical incident that occurred in Bhopal, India, and in Sevesco, Italy, demonstrates what consequence might be. [5]The United States has never experienced great disaster comparable to 1984 Bhopal toxic gas release. [6]When gigantic disaster have occurred in the past, event was often in relatively unpopulated area, and number of casualty caused by incident was limited. [7]Similar incident will undoubtedly occur in future, however, and as American city grow larger, significant mass casualty incident will become more and more possible.

Adapted from *Disaster Medical Assistance Team Organization Guide* (U.S. Department of Defense, 1986), p. 155.

Add either an article (*a, an, the*) or +*s* to the 20 count nouns in the following
paragraph. The verb will often help you decide whether the subject should be
singular (an article) or plural (+*s*).

Urban Trends in the United States

[1]One major urban trend in the United States during last decade has been
growing disparity between resident of central city and suburban portion of
metropolitan area. [2]City and suburb have tended to become increasingly
dissimilar in number of way. [3]Percentage of minority inhabitant in many
central city has increased greatly during the last 50 years, and income level of
central city resident has tended to fall further behind that of suburban dweller.
[4]Growing socioeconomic disparity within metropolitan area stands in sharp
contrast to many decreasing socioeconomic difference between metropolitan
and nonmetropolitan population during the 1970s.

Adapted from "The City-Suburb Income Gap: Is it being Narrowed by a Back-
to-the City Movement?" (Long and Dahmann, 1980), p. 172.

Other Units Related to This Topic

✔ **5.** Definite and Indefinite Meaning for Nouns and Articles

✔ **6.** Generic Meaning for Nouns and Articles

✔ **7.** Noncount Nouns

UNIT 9

Irregular Noun Plurals

Alphabetized List of Irregular Nouns

The following list gives the singular and plural forms of the most common irregular nouns. The list is not complete.

Singular	Plural	Singular	Plural	Singular	Plural
alumnus	alumni	knife	knives	series	series
analysis	analyses	leaf	leaves	sheaf	sheaves
basis	bases	life	lives	sheep	sheep
bass	bass	loaf	loaves	shelf	shelves
calf	calves	man	men	species	species
child	children	matrix	matrices	stimulus	stimuli
crisis	crises		matrixes	syllabus	syllabi
criterion	criteria	means	means		syllabuses
curriculum	curricula	medium	media	synopsis	synopses
	curriculums	memorandum	memoranda	thesis	theses
deer	deer		memorandums	thief	thieves
fish	fish	moose	moose	tooth	teeth
foot	feet	mouse	mice	trout	trout
goose	geese	nucleus	nuclei	vortex	vortices
half	halves	ox	oxen	wife	wives
hoof	hooves	parenthesis	parentheses	wolf	wolves
hypothesis	hypotheses	phenomenon	phenomena	woman	women
index	indices	radius	radii		
	indexes	salmon	salmon		

Regular Forms of Irregular Nouns

Notice that some of the nouns listed in the chart have two possible forms. You need to learn to use the forms that are preferred in your field of study or for the particular meaning that you want to use.

Some irregular nouns have specialized meanings. *Media* is often used to refer to newspapers, magazines, radio, and television as a group.	Representatives of **the media** asked the doctors many questions about the new form of treatment for the flu.
Some nouns have different forms in different contexts. For example, books have *indexes* while economics deals in *indices*.	Her job for the publishing company is to check the **indexes** in all of their books. The economic **indices** suggest that the economy will continue to perform poorly.
Some of these nouns have regular forms that are commonly used. For example, many writers prefer *curriculums*, *memorandums*, and *syllabuses*.	The university requires teachers to give **syllabuses** to their students during the first week of class.

☞ Practice 1

Test your knowledge by giving the plural form for each of these nouns. You might try using each of these in a sentence to check your understanding of their meanings.

1. foot = _____
2. child = _____
3. knife = _____
4. life = _____
5. man = _____

6. mouse = _____
7. parenthesis = _____
8. series = _____
9. wife = _____
10. tooth = _____

Irregular Noun Plurals

☞ Practice 2

Test your knowledge by giving the plural form for each of these nouns. Try using each plural word in a sentence to check your understanding of its meaning.

1. alumnus = _____
2. curriculum = _____
3. hypothesis = _____

4. index = _____
5. memorandum = _____
6. syllabus = _____

☞ Practice 3

Test your knowledge by giving the singular form for each of these plural nouns.

1. analyses = _____
2. children = _____
3. halves = _____
4. wolves = _____
5. teeth = _____

6. geese = _____
7. stimuli = _____
8. sheep = _____
9. vortices = _____
10. radii = _____

Other Units Related to This Topic

✔ **2.** Subject-Verb Agreement

✔**10.** Plural and Singular Forms: Consistency of Use in Writing

UNIT 10

Plural and Singular Forms: Consistency of Use in Writing

Indicating Plural Meaning

1. Nouns. *Count nouns* have both a singular and a plural form. The plural can be regular or irregular.

singular	regular plural
a book	*books*

singular	irregular plural
a child	*children*

2. Pronouns. Personal pronouns have the plural forms *we, us, our, they, them, their,* and *theirs* to refer to plural nouns. *You* and *yours* can be used for either singular or plural meaning.

The students put **their books** under **their desks** before **their teacher** gave them **their final examination.**

We put **our books** under **our desks** before **our teacher** gave us **our final examination.**

3. Determiners. Words such as *these* and *those* can be combined with nouns to show plural meaning along with other meanings.

I bought **these books** at the university bookstore.

The teacher gave **those children** a test.

4. Count words. Numbers and words such as *many* and *a lot of* can be used for plural meanings.

Many people pay their bills with checks.

Two students from Peru showed the other students how to do a traditional dance that they had learned from their grandparents.

5. Noncount nouns. These nouns are neither singular nor plural. They are measured using phrases such as *a lot of, much, a pound of,* and many others. Since they do not have a plural form, +*s* cannot be added.

The cook put **too much salt** on this hamburger.

I bought **a box of salt.**

There is **a pound of salt** in this box.

This salt costs more than **that salt.**

A Note on *None*

While native speakers of English do not always follow this rule consistently, *none* is traditionally considered a singular form for subject-verb agreement. It combines with plural or noncount nouns.

None of the students **was** absent from the test.

None of the information **was** useful for my research project.

Using *Each* and *Every*

Each refers to all members of a group as individuals. *Each* is singular and can be used only with singular nouns.

Students fill out an evaluation of their teachers at the end of **each quarter.**

Each of is used with plural nouns.

Each student gives **her/his** opinion about **each of her/his teachers.**

Every is a synonym of *each.* Both words refer to individuals that are part of a larger group.	**Every student** needs medical insurance.

In informal contexts, the phrase *each and every* is sometimes used for emphasis. It, too, must be with singular nouns.	Each and every student in this class is required to have a copy of the textbook.

Problems with Consistency in Using Plurals

Problem 1

Not using a plural noun with plural words used for counting

Problem	Solution	Revision
*During the war, she took **her two sister** and **her two daughters** to safety.	Both words in a compound noun phrase must have the correct form. Add +s to make the phrase *her two sisters and her two daughters.*	During the war, she took **her two sisters** and **her two daughters** to safety.
*A good teacher needs **these essential characteristic.**	If the writer means one characteristic, then *these* needs to be changed to *this.* If the writer means more than one characteristic, then +s must be added.	A good teacher needs **this essential characteristic.** A good teacher needs **these essential characteristics.**

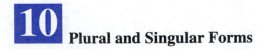

10 **Plural and Singular Forms**

Problem 2

Using incorrect determiners with noncount nouns

Problem	Solution	Revision
*Having **a knowledge** of computers is important for students at this university.	*Knowledge* is a noncount noun. It does not have a singular or a plural form. *A* cannot be used because it means "one," so remove it.	Having **knowledge** of computers is important for students at this university.

Problem 3

Using *each* and *every* with plural nouns rather than with singular nouns

Problem	Solution	Revision
***Each weekends,** people like to have parties with their friends.	*Each* can be used only with a singular noun. Remove the +s to make the phrase *each weekend*.	**Each weekend,** people like to have parties with their friends.
*Teachers cannot help **every students** every day.	*Every* can be used only with a singular noun. Remove the +s to make the phrase *every student*.	Teachers cannot help **every student** every day.

☞ **Practice 1**

Make the noun phrases below correct: add +s where needed. Some phrases do not need changes.

1. three test
2. a well-written book
3. two calculator
4. good advice
5. these essay
6. many library books

7. a lot of money
8. their homework
9. those novel
10. two university team
11. many students
12. one expensive textbook

Plural and Singular Forms 10

13.	two research paper	17.	her book bag
14.	this college	18.	those college credit
15.	several college friend	19.	that university
16.	three class	20.	four short story

☞ **Practice 2**

Add or omit +s to the appropriate nouns; there are 16 changes to make.

1. Smoking in public area should be illegal because it causes a lot of health problem.

2. My college abolished smoking areas several month ago.

3. Many peoples are fascinated by amusement park such as Six Flags and Disney World.

4. Last month, my father took my six friend and me to Six Flags.

5. Just as everyone has daily problem and disappointment, a leader often faces several difficult problem at the same time.

6. A leader needs two essential characteristic: honesty and positive thinking.

7. Self-confidence and charisma are two quality of an effective leader.

8. Every human being has three right: the right of privacy, the right of belief, and the right of speech.

9. Small group discussions in class can make a course interesting; for example, in my political science class we had four discussion group.

10. When teacher establish small group, student often talk more easily in class and become more involved than in a regular class.

Other Units Related to This Topic

✔ 1. Noun-Pronoun Agreement

✔ 2. Subject-Verb Agreement

✔ 4. Avoiding Sexist Language

✔ 7. Noncount Nouns

✔ 9. Irregular Noun Plurals

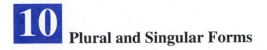

11

The

Summary of the Uses of *The*

Rule 1. *The* is used with some proper nouns. See the list in this unit. Notice that the word *America* does not have an article.

I was born in **the United States**.

America is an ambiguous word. It can refer to **the United States**, or it can refer to all the different countries that are included in **Central, North, and South America**.

Rule 2. *The* can be used with nouns for *definite meaning*. In this meaning, writer and reader share the same information. Singular, plural, and noncount nouns can combine with *the* for definite meaning.

The sun is the center of **the universe**.

I bought **the required textbooks** for this class yesterday.

The water in my glass is cloudy. It seems dirty.

Rule 3. *The* can be used with singular nouns for *generic meaning. The +* singular noun is very frequently used to refer to classes or groups, especially in academic writing. Compare this form with the use of a plural noun without *the* for a similar meaning that is more conversational in tone.

In my opinion, three inventions in the 20th century have changed human life: **the radio, the computer**, and **the air conditioner.**

In my opinion, three inventions in the 20th century have changed human life: **radios, computers,** and **air conditioners.**

The rat can be found in all urban areas.

Rats can be found in all urban areas.

Using *The* with Proper Nouns

Rule 1. Use *the* with the names of the countries and regions on this list. Do not use *the* with the names of other countries.

the Far East
the Middle East
the United Arab Emirates
the United Kingdom
the United States

the Netherlands
the Sudan

Brazil
Greece
India
Paraguay

Rule 2. Use *the* for directional names of regions of countries. Compare the two ways that the adjective forms are used: (1) the southern part of Italy vs. (2) southern Italy.

the North of Kuwait
the South of Italy
the northern part of Kuwait
the southern coast of Italy

northern Kuwait
southern Italy

11 *The*

Rule 3. Use *the* with names for geographical locations: **canals, deserts, forests, oceans, rivers, seas.**

the Panama Canal	*the Atlantic Ocean*
the Sahara Desert	*the Nile River*
the Black Forest	*the Mediterranean Sea*

Rule 4. Use *the* with the names of **islands, lakes, and mountains when the names are plural** in form. Do not use *the* with names of islands, lakes, and mountains when the names are singular in form.

the Great Lakes	*Mount Everest*
the Hawaiian Islands	*Lake Louise*
the Rocky Mountains	*Maui*

Rule 5. Use *the* in the names of universities in the form ***the University of _____***. Generally, universities with other patterns for their names do not use *the*. However, some universities have added *the,* probably to add prestige to their names to sound like the traditional names for state universities. Use whatever name is preferred by the individual institution.

the University of Washington

West Virginia Institute of Technology
Iowa State University

the Florida State University
the Pennsylvania State University

Rule 6. Do not use an article to refer to the names of languages unless the pattern ***the _____ language*** is used. Notice that only the name of the language is capitalized; the word *language* begins with a lowercase letter.

Arabic	*the Arabic language*
English	*the English language*
Greek	*the Greek language*
Italian	*the Italian language*

Problems with *The*

Problem 1

Omitting *the* with certain proper nouns

Problem	Solution	Revision
*I came to **United States** to go to medical school.	*The United States* requires *the*. Add that article.	I came to **the United States** to go to medical school.

The

Problem 2

Using *the* with noncount nouns for generic meaning

Problem	Solution	Revision
*`The water` is necessary for human life.	The writer is talking about water as a substance rather than about particular water. This generic meaning cannot have an article. Remove *the*.	`Water` is necessary for human life.

Problem 3

Using *the* with proper nouns that cannot have an article

Problem	Solution	Revision

*`I came to the America when I was 16 years old.`	The writer seems to have confused two possible names for the United States. *America* cannot have an article. *The United States* must have *the*. Many people from other countries in North and South America prefer the second revision.	`I came to America when I was 16 years old.`
		
		`I came to the United States when I was 16 years old.`

Problem 4

Not using *the* for definite meaning with superlative adjectives

Problem	Solution	Revision
*`"Believe in yourself." That was best advice that I have ever received.`	Superlative forms are used to indicate the top or bottom of a continuum. That meaning requires *the* or some other determiner with definite meaning.	`"Believe in yourself." That was the best advice that I have ever received.`

The

*We have to shop around for **a best computer** at a reasonable price.	As with the first "problem," this sentence needs *the* for definite meaning. Or, the writer could change to a different adjective.	We have to shop around for **the best computer** at a reasonable price.
		We have to shop around for **a good computer** at a reasonable price.

Problem 5

Using *a/an* rather than *the*

Problem	Solution	Revision
*The amount of secondary smoke the rats in the experiment were breathing was **an equivalent of** smoking more than one pack of cigarettes per day.	Generally, the phrase is *the equivalent of.* Change *an* to *the.* Another similar phrase is *equivalent to.*	The amount of secondary smoke the rats in the experiment were breathing was **the equivalent of** smoking more than one pack of cigarettes per day.
		The amount of secondary smoke the rats in the experiment were breathing was **equivalent to** smoking more than one pack of cigarettes per day.

☹ Sometimes the 20th century is called **an age of computers.**

The "problem" sentence has a strange meaning because it says that there are many ages of computers. A more likely meaning is that there is only one age of computers; change *an* to *the*.

Sometimes the 20th century is called **the age of computers.**

☛ Practice 1

Add *the* to the following proper nouns, where needed.

1.	_____ America	11.	_____ Rocky Mountains
2.	_____ Andes Mountains	12.	_____ Sahara Desert
3.	_____ Arctic Ocean	13.	_____ South America
4.	_____ Augustana College	14.	_____ Spanish language
5.	_____ Hong Kong	15.	_____ Suez Canal
6.	_____ Indonesia	16.	_____ United States
7.	_____ Italy	17.	_____ University of Wyoming
8.	_____ Latin	18.	_____ Utah
9.	_____ Missouri River	19.	_____ Venezuela
10.	_____ Philippine Islands	20.	_____ Wales

☛ Practice 2

Add *the*, where necessary, to the following sentences. Some sentences need more than one change, and some sentences are correct.

1. Six students in my class are from South America, and ten are from Asia.

2. North of United States is often colder than South.

3. I lived in Greece for three years and traveled to many Greek islands.

4. Although many languages are spoken in Far East, only one language is generally spoken in Middle East.

11 *The*

5. Southern California is usually more humid than northern California.

6. I spent three weeks last summer on a yacht sailing on Mediterranean Sea.

7. Mississippi River is longest river in United States.

8. I plan to transfer either to University of California or University of Nevada.

9. My roommate has studied Spanish language for five years but has never visited Spain or South America.

10. My favorite Hawaiian island is Maui, but I enjoy visiting all of Hawaiian Islands.

☛ **Practice 3**

Choose the correct answer to each question. Then, add *the*, if needed.

1. _____ are the mountains in Kentucky. (Alps Mountains, Appalachian Mountains, Rocky Mountains)

2. _____ lies between England and Norway. (Black Sea, Mediterranean Sea, North Sea)

3. _____ flows through Paris. (Danube River, Rhine River, Seine River)

4. Honolulu is the capital of _____. (Hawaii, Japan, Philippine Islands)

5. Ecuador is located in _____. (Asia, North America, South America)

6. _____ is located in the United States. (Erie Canal, Panama Canal, Suez Canal)

7. _____ language is the main language in Ireland. (English, French, German)

8. The capital of Spain is _____. (Athens, Madrid, Rome)

9. _____ is located between the United States and Japan. (Atlantic Ocean, Indian Ocean, Pacific Ocean)

10. _____ is located between Germany and Italy. (Japan, Panama, Switzerland)

The

☛ Practice 4

Add *the* to the following sentences. Make any necessary corrections to the sentences.

1. In United States, high schools seem very different from those in my country.

2. English 101 is an enjoyable class for me because the teacher of class is excellent.

3. Most students arrive in classroom at 7:45 in morning.

4. In order to improve my vocabulary, I should use an English-English dictionary rather than bilingual dictionary that I currently use.

5. English 101 is hardest class that I have ever taken; class is challenging and time-consuming.

Other Units Related to This Topic

✔ **3.** *A* and *An*

✔ **5.** Definite and Indefinite Meaning for Nouns and Articles

✔ **6.** Generic Meaning for Nouns and Articles

✔ **7.** Noncount Nouns

✔ **8.** Nouns Without Articles

 11 *The*

SECTION

III

Conditional and Hypothetical Meaning

Conditional Sentences

Definition of *Conditional Sentence*

Conditional sentences present relationships in which something is necessary to cause something else to happen. If one thing happens, the other thing is usually guaranteed to happen.

Students will learn more if their professors talk clearly and are well-prepared for class.

Meaning of Conditional Sentences

General Truth Conditions. Generalizations can be made in the form of conditional sentences. In these sentences, *if* means "when" or "under these conditions." *Will* and *can* are used for the meanings of "certainty" and "possibility" but without any future time meaning. The verb in the *if*-clause is in the simple present tense.

Water boils if it reaches 212 degrees F.

Water will boil if it reaches 212 degrees F.

Students can attend the concert for free if they present their university identification at the entrance.

Future Time Conditions. Conditional sentences can be about future events. The verb in the *if*-clause is in the simple present tense. The verb in the main clause has a future time meaning and is usually formed with one of the modal auxiliary verbs.

```
If they take psychology
next quarter, they will
graduate in the summer.

More new cars should be
sold this year if the
economy continues to
improve.
```

Past Time Conditions. Conditional statements can be made about relationships between events in the past. The verb in the *if*-clause and the main verb are in the simple past tense.

```
Last year I took a very
difficult economics course.
If I made a good grade on a
quiz, I was very happy.

George Washington lived
before electricity was
harnessed for power. If he
wanted to talk with his
advisers, he visited with
them in person or wrote
them letters. He could not
call on the telephone or
send a FAX.
```

Problems with Conditional Sentences

Problem 1

Creating a statement that is not logical or not convincing

Problem	Solution	Revision
☹ If a person **dresses** well in expensive clothes, then that person **is rich.**	This statement seems too strong. People can buy expensive clothes in second-hand shops or receive them as gifts or buy them on credit or make them themselves. A more tentative statement might be made by using other wording such as using a modal auxiliary verb with tentative meaning.	If a person **dresses** well in expensive clothes, then that person **presents** a successful appearance. If a person **dresses** well in expensive clothes, then that person **might possibly be** rich.

Conditional Sentences

Confusing conditional with hypothetical sentences

Problem	Solution	Revision
*If professors **know** their weaknesses through student evaluations, they **would change** the way they teach.	Conditional sentences are used to make statements that are strong predictions of truth. Hypothetical statements are more tentative and even impossible. This writer is making a very strong statement that if one thing happens, the other thing will certainly result. The *if*-clause is in the conditional form with the present tense verb. The main clause is in the hypothetical form with *would*. To make the sentence conditional, change to *will*.	If professors **know** their weaknesses through student evaluations, they **will change** the way they teach.

☞ **Practice 1**

Complete each of the following to make a conditional statement.

1. If water is chilled to 0 degrees centigrade, it_____.

2. If a student course evaluation shows a problem in a class, _____.

3. If a student receives a low grade on a test, s/he_____.

4. This university requires 550 on TOEFL. If a student makes 560 on TOEFL, s/he
   _____.

5. I am taking a writing class. If I pass the final examination, _____.

6. If a student wears a business suit to class,_____.

7. When I was a child, if I did not like my father's advice,_____.

☛ Practice 2

Correct the verbs, if necessary, in the following conditional sentences.

1. If professors are told their weaknesses in student evaluations, most would change the way that they teach.

2. If administrators take student evaluations seriously, the school will benefit.

3. Students would learn more if professors talk clearly and are well prepared for class.

4. If students are allowed to select their own courses, they would be forced to learn about core courses and major requirements.

5. At most universities, if a student will cheat on an exam, that student will receive a zero on the exam.

☛ Practice 3

Correct the verbs, if necessary, in the following conditional sentences.

1. If people learn self-discipline when they were children, they would not have problems when they are adults.

2. If people are organized, they would be successful.

3. If I win a million dollars in a lottery, I will go to a more prestigious university.

4. If office workers are exposed to an office filled with smoke for eight hours every day, some of them would have eventually suffered from lung cancer.

5. Some people continue to smoke because they think they will gain weight if they quit smoking.

6. If the United States allows the importing of foreign cars, the customers received many advantages.

7. If the United States will limit its consumers to American cars, the customers will be the losers.

8. Most university teachers announce their policy on plagiarism early in the quarter, and if a student cheats, that student would face serious problems.

9. If a student tries to cheat during an exam, that student should be dismissed from the school.

10. Juan said to Carlos, "If you have no knowledge of computers, you might as well be living in the stone age."

12   **Conditional Sentences**   **77**

☛ **Practice 4**

Make statements about conditional relationships that you know about. Two examples are given as models. In these conditional statements, one thing causes another thing.

1. If water is heated to 212 degrees F., it boils.

2. If water is chilled to 32 degrees F., it will freeze.

3. _____

4. _____

5. _____

6. _____

7. _____

8. _____

9. _____

10. _____

Other Units Related to This Topic

✔**13.** Hypothetical Sentences

Hypothetical Sentences

Definition of *Hypothetical Sentence*

Hypothetical sentences are used to discuss things that are not true or that did not happen. Hypothetical events are imaginary events. The writer is saying "This is not true, but isn't it interesting to think about?"

If Mohammad Ali **had been** a professor rather than a boxer, he **would have given** eloquent lectures. He **could have used** his mind rather than his body to make a living.

Hypothetical statements are used in academic writing and academic discussions as a method for raising issues and for evaluating ideas.

Think about the problem this way. If the government both **raised** taxes on gasoline and **created** better public transportation, people **would be** more likely to use public transportation than private cars. However, if the government **raised** gasoline taxes without providing better public transportation, people **would find** it difficult to get to work.

While hypothetical and conditional sentences have similar grammar, they are very different in meaning. Conditional sentences are statements of reality used to explain how one thing causes another thing. Hypothetical sentences show imagined, unreal relationships.

conditional statement

If a student **checks** a book out of the library, s/he **must return** it in three weeks. If at the end of that time s/he still **needs** the book, it **can be rechecked** for another three weeks.

hypothetical statement

Because he was in his forties when he died, we think of John F. Kennedy as a young man. However, if he **were** alive today, he **would be** an old man.

Meaning and Grammar of Hypothetical Sentences

General Truth. In these statements, untrue situations are used to discuss issues and problems. The verb in the *if*-clause is simple past tense. The verb in the main clause will generally use either *would* or *could.* Past tense verbs are used for a special meaning; they do not refer to past time in such sentences.

He does not know how to type, and he cannot be a student assistant.

If he **knew** how to type, he **could be** a student assistant.

Past Time. Hypothetical sentences are often used to talk about things that failed to happen in the past. The *if*-clause is used to state something that did not happen. The main clause tells the results. The *if*-clause uses a past perfect verb form. The main clause uses a modal perfect—modal + *have* + past participle. Generally, the modal will be either *would* or *could,* but *should, might,* and *must* can also be used. Notice the use of the negative in the *if*-clause in the second example.

We did not study the details very carefully. We did buy the insurance. Both events happened in the past.

If we **had studied** the details of the policy more carefully, we **would not have bought** this medical insurance.

The teacher listened. The test was changed to another day.

If our grammar teacher **had not listened** to our suggestions, we **would have had** a test on a day that is an important religious holiday in our culture.

Past Time Influencing Present Time.
Past time events can influence the present. The verb in the *if*-clause is a past perfect form; the main verb combines modal + verb.

I did not take college algebra in the past, so I cannot take calculus in the present.

If I **had taken** college algebra last year, I **could take** calculus now.

The writer got a scholarship in the past and is attending the university in the present.

If the university **had not given** a scholarship, I **would not be** at this school because the tuition is so high.

Were in Hypothetical Sentences

In formal spoken and written English, the form of *be* in a hypothetical *if*-clause is *were* for all subjects. Some grammarians call this use of *were* the subjunctive. Notice that this use of the subjunctive occurs only in general truth, present time statements.

The weather is bad.

If the weather **were** better, we **could play** tennis.

The teacher is not here.

If the teacher **were** here, class **would begin.**

Thomas Edison is dead.

If Thomas Edison **were** alive, he **would want** a computer.

A frequently used phrase for giving advice is "If I were you, I would. . . ."

If I **were** you, I **would talk** with our teacher about your problem.

If I **were** you, I **would sell** that old car and **buy** a bicycle.

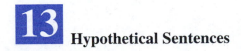

Problem		

Not using the correct verb forms consistently in writing on hypothetical topics

Problem	Solution	Revision
*If I **were** to lose my hearing, I **will be** very sad because I **can no longer hear** the voices of my friends.	The writer is making a hypothetical response to a question about which of his/her five senses s/he would most hate to lose. The statement needs to be completely hypothetical. The verbs must be changed to past forms and to *would* or *could* to indicate that this is not a conditional statement.	If I **were** to lose my hearing, I **would be** very sad because I **could no longer hear** the voices of my friends.

☛ **Practice 1**

Correct the verbs, if necessary, in the following hypothetical sentences.

1. If I won a million dollars in a lottery, my life would change very much mentally, economically, and socially.

2. I always think that if I was rich, I could change my life.

3. The first step I will take if I won a lottery is I will sit and think wisely about how to use this money.

4. If I had a million dollars, the first thing I will do is open a restaurant because that is a dream of mine.

5. If I won a lottery, I will live in my country, and I will be respected by many people.

☛ **Practice 2**

Correct the verbs, if necessary, in the following hypothetical sentences.

1. If I lived in my country and I had lots of money, my life would be changed economically.

2. Ten years ago, my country was not economically stable, but if I had money then, I would invest all my money in real estate.

3. If I didn't come to the U.S., my life is much better than right now.

4. I thought that I will learn English automatically if I move to the U.S., but now I am having a difficult time learning English.

5. If I learn to speak English in my country, I will not have problems talking to Americans.

6. If I could change one thing about my childhood, I would like to stay in my country until I graduate from high school.

7. If I had taken time out to become more involved in my high school studies, perhaps I would be smarter today.

8. If I was a smoker, I would get angry at anyone who came to me and said, "Don't smoke because it is not good for your health."

9. If his teachers had paid more attention to his cheating, he wouldn't have done it so often.

10. I am not here in this college if I won a lottery.

☞ Practice 3

Edit the following paragraph for hypothetical verbs. Make seven changes.

A Million Dollars: How It Would Change My Life

¹Today, a million dollars is not enough to change some people's lives dramatically. ²However, a million dollars is still a lot of money for me, so it would change my life. ³First of all, I would buy a brand-new car that will give me reliable transportation and a convenient lifestyle. ⁴Secondly, I will invest in myself and use some of the money for my education. ⁵I want to get a degree and begin a career in medicine. ⁶The final thing that I will change is my lifestyle. ⁷Because of the million dollars, I do not have to be worried about living expenses and can have a more stable life. ⁸I will also be independent from my father in Japan. ⁹These are the ways that my life would be changed if I won a million dollars. ¹⁰People may say that money cannot buy happiness, but I think that I can be happy with convenience, stability, and confidence.

☞ Practice 4

The following essay combines hypothetical with general truth writing. First, mark the section of the essay that uses general truth forms for a series of questions. The rest of the essay should be hypothetical. Second, edit the whole essay for consistency in form to be sure that the correct hypothetical and general truth forms are used.

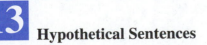

13 **Hypothetical Sentences** 83

Teacher Evaluation

[1]If I were asked to evaluate my teachers, I would use standards that were based first on their interest in teaching and their knowledge of the subject. [2]I would prepared a list of questions with a number scale from one to five. [3]The number five would be very positive, and the number one will be negative. [4]The numbers in between would be moderate depending on the end they fell close to on the scale.

[5]Once I had the number scale finish, I would filled in the questions to be answered about each teacher:

1. How well does the teacher knows the material for the course?

2. Does the teacher asked the students if they understood the material?

3. Is the teacher well prepared each day for class?

4. Does the teacher really likes the subject?

[6]All these questions would go under the categories of "interest in teaching" and "knowledge of subject matter." [7]In addition to these questions, I would also asked if the professor were biased, using the following question:

5. Does the professor discriminates either because a student was born in a different country or is of a different race or is smarter than other students?

[8]All these questions would be evaluated on the number scale. [9]For each question, I would circle the appropriate number which I thinked best described a particular teacher. [10]Once I had the number circled for each question, I would counted the points for each question and figured an average total score. [11]Using these numbers, I would be able to evaluating all of my teachers to provide information about my opinions on their teaching skills. [12]This information will be of use to the teachers and to the administrators as a method for improving the quality of teaching at this school.

Other Units Related to This Topic

✔**12.** Conditional Sentences

✔**36.** Subjunctive Verbs

Hypothetical Sentences **13**

SECTION

IV

Coordination

Coordinating Conjunctions

Some students use the made-up word *fanboys* as a mnemonic device to help them remember the coordinating conjunctions that are used with a comma to create a compound sentence.

F	*for*	English is studied by more people than any other language, **for** it has become the language of business, tourism, science, and diplomacy.
A	*and*	Jose is majoring in physics, **and** his brother is studying art history.
N	*nor*	I have never visited Venezuela, **nor** do I have much hope of going there soon.
B	*but*	Liliana studied calculus in high school, **but** she will be required to take it again here at the university.
O	*or*	In this course students can write a research paper, **or** they can take a final examination.
Y	*yet*	We have worked very hard on this project, **yet** we are not certain that our work will be rewarded.
S	*so*	The final examination will be on Monday, **so** I must study this weekend rather than play soccer.

The Many Meanings of *And*

ADDITION	She is taking calculus, and she is also studying physics.
RESULT	She studied hard for the test, and as a result she was well prepared for the questions.
TIME	They went to the library, and then they went to the computer laboratory.
CONTRAST	Maria is happy about her test results, and Margaret is unhappy about hers.
COMMENT	I do not like history, and that is the truth.
CONDITION	Help me study for the math test, and I will help you study for the English test.

 **Practice 1**

Without looking at the FANBOYS chart, write the coordinating conjunction that each letter stands for. Then write an example of a sentence that uses that word. Check the punctuation of each example sentence carefully.

1. F = _____ _____

2. A = _____ _____

3. N = _____ _____

4. B = _____ _____

5. O = _____ _____

6. Y = _____ _____

7. S = _____ _____

☞ Practice 2

Because *and* has so many meanings, it is often better to use a more exact word or to add a transition word or phrase to make the meaning clear. Revise each of the following sentences to make its meaning more exact. The first one is done for you as an example. Three possible revisions are shown to remind you that you have various choices. Be careful to use correct punctuation.

1. For most English speakers, Spanish is easy to learn, and Japanese is very difficult to learn.

   REVISION 1: For most English speakers, Spanish is easy to learn, but Japanese is very difficult to learn.

   REVISION 2: For most English speakers, Spanish is easy to learn while Japanese is very difficult to learn.

   REVISION 3: For most English speakers, Spanish is easy to learn; however, Japanese is very difficult to learn.

2. My roommate likes rap, and I like classical Indian music.

3. I went to class, and I went home to study for my final exam.

4. My physics teacher realized that we did not understand the problem, and she gave us another example.

5. Jose locked his keys in his car, and he called the campus police for help.

☞ Practice 3

Like *and,* the other coordinating conjunctions have more than one meaning. Look up these words in an English-English dictionary for examples of their uses.

Other Units Related to This Topic

Coordinating Conjunctions

UNIT **15**

Compound Sentences

Compound Sentence Defined

A *compound sentence* is a combination of two or more simple sentences.

Usually the combination is made using a comma with one of the coordinating conjunctions.

simple sentence #1
```
Water is necessary for all
life.
```

simple sentence # 2
```
Human beings are destroying
the world's water supply.
```

compound sentence
```
Water is necessary for all
life, but human beings are
destroying the world's
water supply.
```

Also, semicolons can be used to make compound sentences. A transition word is often added when a semicolon is used to make the relationship between the two parts of the sentence clear.

```
Water is necessary for all
life; however, human beings
are destroying the world's
water supply.
```

89

☞ Practice 1

Analyze the sentence types in the following paragraph: you should find five compound sentences (_____, _____, _____, _____, _____,) and one compound-complex sentence (_____). You should find other types of coordination in the four other sentences (_____, _____, _____, and _____).

My Family

[1]After living with my family for twenty-one years, I recently moved and experienced the feeling of being far away from my brothers and sisters. [2]My brothers and sisters, even now, help me feel warm and not lonely; they make me feel happy.   [3]I have eight brothers and sisters; being a part of this large family, I have never felt lonely. [4]When I was a child, my brothers and sisters helped me solve my problems, and today we often share our happiness or sadness by sending letters or by making phone calls. [5]For example, my oldest sister helped me adjust after my move to college, and she still gives me advice about how to deal with problems that I have. [6]Likewise, I enjoy helping my youngest sister and giving her advice. [7]She sends me letters, and we talk on the telephone about twice a month. [8]She tells me about her new friends and about how she is doing in school. [9]Sometimes, I wonder how I would feel if I didn't have brothers and sisters. [10]I think that the most important thing in life is being a part of a family, that having many brothers and sisters is one of the great pleasures in life.

☞ Practice 2

Analyze the sentence types in the following paragraph: sentences _____, _____, and _____ are simple; sentences _____, _____, and _____ are compound; sentences _____ and _____ are complex; sentences _____ and _____ are compound-complex.

The Pleasures of Being a Mathematics Tutor

[1]I enjoyed tutoring mathematics to high school students two years ago because I had a chance to encourage and support students who were weak, unorganized, and lazy. [2]I had three groups of students, and each group had four students. [3]I tutored each group five days a week for about two to three hours. [4]Some students were very weak in mathematics, so I needed to spend extra time with them: reviewing the chapters that they were studying, helping them solve problems, and explaining mathematical theories. [5]Some of the other students were unorganized and lazy; for example, they did not do homework, and they did not always review for exams. [6]They had previously studied only the day before the test; in other words, they had only prepared the last twenty-four hours before any test in the past. [7]I tried to teach them how to

deal with their laziness. [8]For example, they needed to solve all the problems that were assigned as homework, and they needed to spend at least two hours every day on their math homework. [9]After two months of tutoring, they started getting good grades on their tests. [10]In short, I liked being a tutor because I could help the students understand math better and also help them get better grades.

Other Units Related to This Topic

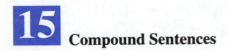 **Compound Sentences**

SECTION

V

+*ing* Words and Infinitives

16

Gerunds

Using Gerunds in Sentences

A *gerund* is an *+ing* form of a verb used in the same ways as a noun in a sentence. The verb *walk* is changed by adding *+ing*. The new word *walking* is used as the subject of the example sentence.

verb
I **walk** to work every morning.

gerund
Walking is my favorite sport.

Gerunds are used in five different ways in sentences: subject, direct object, complement, object of a preposition, and appositive.

Notice that these are all noun functions: the gerund is used in the same ways that nouns are used in sentences.

1. gerund as subject
Walking is my favorite sport.

2. gerund as direct object
I like **walking.**

3. gerund as complement
My favorite sport is **walking.**

4. gerund as object of preposition
I look forward to **walking** to work.

5. gerund as appositive
My favorite sport, **walking,** does not require any special equipment.

Verbs That Have Gerunds as Their Objects

The following verbs require a gerund rather than an infinitive as their direct objects.

He avoids **playing** card games.

The teacher postponed **giving** the test.

admit	describe	imagine	protest
advise	despise	include	recall
anticipate	detest	increase	recommend
appreciate	discuss	involve	regret
avoid	enjoy	keep	report
be used to	escape	mention	resent
be worth	excuse	mind	resist
can(not) help	finish	miss	risk
complete	forbid	object to	suggest
consider	forgive	postpone	tolerate
defer	get through	practice	understand
delay	get used to	prevent	
deny	give up		

Verbs That Have Gerunds or Infinitives as Their Objects with Different Meanings

The following verbs can have either a gerund or an infinitive as their direct objects, but the two versions have different meanings.

He does not smoke anymore.

He stopped **smoking.**

He stopped walking to do something. He smoked a cigarette.

Walking to class, he stopped **to smoke** a cigarette.

forget   mean   need   propose   quit   regret   remember   stop   want

Verbs That Have Gerunds or Infinitives as Their Objects with the Same Meaning

The following verbs can have either a gerund or an infinitive as their direct objects. Both versions have the same meaning.

He hates **to swim.**

He hates **swimming.**

attempt	*continue*	*like*	*plan*	*start*
begin	*dread*	*love*	*prefer*	*try*
bother	*hate*	*neglect*	*propose*	
can't stand	*intend*	*permit*	*stand*	

Problems with Gerunds

Problem 1

Using an infinitive rather than a gerund after a preposition

Problem	Solution	Revision
*I **look forward to meet** you when you arrive next week.	The word *to* in the phrase *look forward to* is a preposition. The preposition *to* must be followed by a gerund rather than an infinitive.	I **look forward to meeting** you when you arrive next week.
*Reza passed the test **after take** a test preparation course. He gained confidence **by study** many practice tests.	*After* can be either a preposition or a subordinating conjunction. *By* is a preposition. The writer has two choices for this revision.	*after* as a preposition Reza passed the test **after taking** a test preparation course. He gained confidence **by studying** many practice tests.

Reza passed the
test **after he took**
a test preparation
course. He gained
confidence **by**
studying many
practice tests.

Problem 2

Not having correct subject-verb agreement

Problem	Solution	Revision
*Having many children cost a lot of money.	Remember the general rule: if a subject is not clearly plural, then treat it as singular. Add +*s* to the verb.	Having many children costs a lot of money.

Problem 3

Not using the plural form of certain gerunds

Problem	Solution	Revision
*I think that we **human being** are often lazy. *A school should consider **the feeling** of its students.	Most gerunds are noncount nouns. However, a few gerunds have become count nouns; they have both a singular and a plural form.	I think that we **human beings** are often lazy. A school should consider **the feelings** of its students.

a human being	*human beings*
a feeling	*the feelings*

 **Gerunds**

Problem 4

Not using the correct pronoun form in formal writing for the subject of a gerund

Problem	Solution	Revision
*Our teacher complained about **us talking** so much in class.	In formal writing, the subject of the gerund needs to be a possessive form. The gerund is based on the following sentence: *We talk so much in class.* Change *us* to *our.* (The "problem" version can be used in informal contexts.)	Our teacher complained about **our talking** so much in class.
*The president explained the reasons for **him recommending** that tuition be raised.	The gerund is based on the following sentence: *He recommended that tuition be raised.* The subject of the gerund needs to be in the possessive form. Change *him* to *his.* (The "problem" version could be used in informal contexts.)	The president explained the reasons for **his recommending** that tuition be raised.
*The president explained the reasons for the **university raising** its tuition.	The gerund is based on the following sentence: *The university raised its tuition.* The subject of the gerund needs to be changed to the possessive form. Add *'s* to *the university.* (The "problem" version could be used in informal contexts.)	The president explained the reasons for **the university's** raising its tuition.

Gerunds  16

☞ Practice 1

When you see the following verbs, should a gerund or an infinitive follow? Circle the correct response. Some verbs below can have either a gerund or an infinitive as their objects. Try writing a sentence using each verb.

1. *can help*	+	(gerund) (infinitive)	**11.** *avoid* + (gerund) (infinitive)
2. *enjoy*	+	(gerund) (infinitive)	**12.** *prefer* + (gerund) (infinitive)
3. *like*	+	(gerund) (infinitive)	**13.** *afford* + (gerund) (infinitive)
4. *hope*	+	(gerund) (infinitive)	**14.** *imagine* + (gerund) (infinitive)
5. *arrange*	+	(gerund) (infinitive)	**15.** *postpone* + (gerund) (infinitive)
6. *continue*	+	(gerund) (infinitive)	**16.** *try* + (gerund) (infinitive)
7. *hesitate*	+	(gerund) (infinitive)	**17.** *attempt* + (gerund) (infinitive)
8. *manage*	+	(gerund) (infinitive)	**18.** *recommend* + (gerund) (infinitive)
9. *promise*	+	(gerund) (infinitive)	**19.** *stop* + (gerund) (infinitive)
10. *quit*	+	(gerund) (infinitive)	**20.** *expect* + (gerund) (infinitive)

☞ Practice 2

Replace infinitives and verbs with gerunds in the following sentences to make the sentences correct. Some sentences need two corrections.

1. I think that self-discipline means coming to class on time every day and work extra hours to complete an assignment.

2. Many students become impatient when they start do things that are new and difficult for them.

3. I need to stop to expect that the money my parents send will arrive early; I need to start budget my money.

4. My roommate enjoys jogging before classes and swim after classes in the university pool.

5. I started look for a part-time job last month because I wanted to buy a car, but I stopped to look after a month because there were no part-time jobs within walking distance of my dorm.

6. My advisor keeps tell me that I should look for a job on campus.

7. I realize that I should not consider quit college until I complete my degree and can get a job with security and benefits rather than a job that is temporary.

8. My father began learn English when he was 46 years old; he is 62 now.

16 **Gerunds**

9. He has attempted to speak better, but so far he has continued speak Spanish at home every day.

10. I have learned from my father that it is very difficult for adults to learn a second language; sometimes a person cannot help speak a native language even when that person wants to change.

☞ Practice 3

Read the following paragraph, and write the correct form of the verb in parentheses on the appropriate line. If no correction is necessary, leave the line blank. If you would like to review the use of infinitives, turn to Unit 22.

The Assembly Line

Henry Ford pioneered in [1](improve) assembly line methods [2](cut) production costs. His goal was [3](lower) the price of cars so that everyone could afford [4](buy) a car. In 1908, Ford achieved his goal with the Model T, which sold for $850. In 1913, Ford installed an assembly line in his factory. As the frame of a car moved on a conveyor belt, workers on each side assembled the car by [5](add) parts that had been brought to them by other conveyor belts. In 1914, Ford workers were able [6](build) a Model T in a little more than an hour and a half. [7](Build) the earlier Model T had taken about 12 1/2 hours. By [8](save) 11 hours of production costs, the 1916 Model T could be sold for less than $400. Ford sold over 15 million Model T's from 1908–1917, and more than half the automobiles sold in America between 1908 and 1917 were Fords.

1._____   5._____

2._____   6._____

3._____   7._____

4._____   8._____

Information adapted from *World Book Encyclopedia,* 1988 ed.

Other Units Related to This Topic

✔ **2.** Subject-Verb Agreement

✔ **17.** Infinitives

✔ **18.** Overview of +*ing* Words

Gerunds  **16**

Infinitives

Using Infinitives in Sentences

Infinitive is the name for the basic form of the verb, for example, *to walk.* Teachers and grammar books may also use the term *infinitive* for the form without *to* when it is used with an auxiliary to make a complete verb phrase in a sentence.

Infinitives are used in six different ways in English sentences: subject, direct object, complement, appositive, adjective modifier, and adverbial.

full infinitive
He likes **to walk** to class.

bare infinitive
He will **walk** to class.

1. infinitive as subject
To love is not the same as to be loved.

2. infinitive as direct object
Maritza wants **to study** astrophysics.

3. infinitive as complement
To know him is **to love** him.

4. infinitive as appositive
Her plan, **to study astrophysics,** pleases her family.

5. infinitive as adjective modifier
She is very **happy to have** her family's support for her plan.

6. infinitive as adverbial
She came to the United States **to study astrophysics.**

101

Verbs That Have Infinitives as Their Objects

The following verbs require an infinitive rather than a gerund as their direct object. See Unit 16 on "Gerunds" for lists of verbs that require gerunds or that can have either gerunds or infinitives as their objects.

problem

*He **agreed studying** in the library after class.

revision

He **agreed to study** in the library after class.

Many of these verbs can also be used in complex sentences that put clauses in the direct object. In this example, two sentences are combined. The gerund is the subject of the dependent noun clause.

He agreed that....

Studying in the library was a good plan.

combination with *that*

He agreed that <u>studying in the library</u> <u>was</u> a good plan.

combination without *that*

He agreed <u>studying in the library</u> <u>was</u> a good plan.

The following is a list of verbs that can take the infinitive form in the object position.

afford	*consent*	*go*	*neglect*	*request*
agree	*decide*	*happen*	*prepare*	*say*
appear	*demand*	*hesitate*	*pretend*	*seem*
ask	*deserve*	*hope*	*proceed*	*struggle*
beg	*desire*	*intend*	*promise*	*swear*
care	*endeavor*	*learn*	*prove*	*wait*
claim	*expect*	*manage*	*refuse*	*wish*
come	*fail*			

Problem 1

Using an infinitive when a gerund is needed

Problem	Solution	Revision
*I **want studying** chemistry.	The verb *want* needs an infinitive in its direct object for this meaning.	I **want to study** chemistry.

Problem 2

Using a base form where a complete infinitive is needed

Problem	Solution	Revision
*I **want study** chemistry.	The complete infinitive is required. Add *to.*	I **want to study** chemistry.

Problem 3

Using an +*ing* form when an infinitive is needed

Problem	Solution	Revision
*I cannot find time **to traveling.**	The writer has two choices: (1) since *to* marks an infinitive, remove +*ing*. (2) Remove *to,* and add the preposition *for.*	I cannot find time **to travel.** I cannot find time **for traveling.**
*He started **to smoking and drinking** alcohol.	*Start* can have either an infinitive or a gerund, but the writer must decide on one or the other. Both choices are shown in the revisions.	He started **to smoke and to drink** alcohol. He started **smoking and drinking** alcohol.

Infinitives

Problem 4

Using the wrong infinitive form with a modal auxiliary

Problem	Solution	Revision
*In the 21st century, the United Nations **will to need** more health services for children in developing countries.	A modal auxiliary is followed by the simple form of the verb. Remove *to*.	In the 21st century, the United Nations **will need** more health services for children in developing countries.

☞ Practice 1

When you see the following verbs, should an infinitive or a gerund follow? Circle the correct response. Some verbs below can have either an infinitive or a gerund as their objects. Try to write a sentence using each verb.

1. *attempt*	+ (gerund) (infinitive)	11. *avoid*	+ (gerund) (infinitive)
2. *imagine*	+ (gerund) (infinitive)	12. *afford*	+ (gerund) (infinitive)
3. *promise*	+ (gerund) (infinitive)	13. *hesitate*	+ (gerund) (infinitive)
4. *quit*	+ (gerund) (infinitive)	14. *enjoy*	+ (gerund) (infinitive)
5. *agree*	+ (gerund) (infinitive)	15. *stop*	+ (gerund) (infinitive)
6. *hope*	+ (gerund) (infinitive)	16. *postpone*	+ (gerund) (infinitive)
7. *promise*	+ (gerund) (infinitive)	17. *expect*	+ (gerund) (infinitive)
8. *recommend*	+ (gerund) (infinitive)	18. *prefer*	+ (gerund) (infinitive)
9. *arrange*	+ (gerund) (infinitive)	19. *like*	+ (gerund) (infinitive)
10. *continue*	+ (gerund) (infinitive)	20. *manage*	+ (gerund) (infinitive)

Infinitives

☞ Practice 2

Correct the problems with gerunds and infinitives in the following sentences. There may be more than one revision in a sentence.

1. I also plan earning a degree as soon as I can to afford go to college as a full-time student; lottery money would help me go to college.

2. If I do not win the lottery, I will to have work and save money for my education.

3. I enjoy traveling and want traveling around the world after I graduate.

4. Many people buy lottery tickets every day because they hope strike it rich.

5. I am one of those people who would like win a lot of money and not have to go to college.

☞ Practice 3

Read the following paragraph, and correct each verb and infinitive.

My New Job

¹My first day of work at the Ames Machine Shop was difficult because I had to meet new people, to followed new rules, and to learn a new skill. ²Since everybody is new to me, I also have to get to know people and had to introduced myself to the other workers. ³I had to watched and learned how to work different machines and to used different tools. ⁴The morning seem very long and frustrating because I did not knowed how to do my job and because I felt uncomfortable. ⁵However, as I worked through the day, I become more relaxed and more comfortable with the job and with myself. ⁶The second day I return to work with a smile, and I am ready learn more about my new job..

Other Units Related to This Topic

Infinitives

Overview of +*ing* Words

Three Uses of Verbs Ending with +*ing*

Progressive Verbs. Progressive verbs are formed with *be* followed by a verb +*ing*. The verb in each sentence is underlined with two lines.

The student is complaining about the cost of insurance.

The students were complaining about the increase in tuition.

Present Participles. The +*ing* form of a verb is called a *participle* when it is used in a verb phrase or when it is used as an adjective. This form is often called the *present participle*. The subject of the sentence is underlined with one line.

The complaining student wanted to talk with the president of the university.

Gerunds. The +*ing* form of a verb is called a *gerund* when it is used as a noun in a sentence. In this example, the gerund is the subject of the sentence.

Complaining is usually unpleasant but sometimes necessary.

Two Kinds of Participles as Adjectives

The term *participle* is used for the +*ing* form of a verb and also for the past participle of the verb. These two participles have very different meanings. In general, the +*ing* participle (also called the *present participle*) refers to something the noun is doing or causing. On the other hand, the *past participle* refers to something that has been done to the noun; the past participle has a passive meaning.

+*ing* participle/present participle

The **speeding** car ran off the road.

past participle of a regular verb

The cook put the **sliced** chicken on the sandwich.

past participle of an irregular verb

The **stolen** car was never found.

Problems With Verbs Ending With +*ing*

Problem 1

Not spelling the +*ing* form correctly

Problem	Solution	Revision
*Reading and **writing** lead to improved communication skills so that people can understand each other better.	The +*ing* form of the verb *write* is *writing*.	Reading and **writing** lead to improved communication skills so that people can understand each other better.

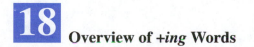

Confusing +*ing* adjectives (present participles) with past participles

Problem	Solution	Revision
☹ This book is very **interested**.	Some students make frequent use of the words *boring/bored* and *interesting/interested*. These words can be a problem because incorrect use can lead to puzzling and humorous sentences. The past participles refer to actions received or felt by a person or other living being. A book cannot feel anything.	This book is very **interesting**. **This interesting book** is required for my history course. I am very **interested** in **this interesting book**.
☹ I am very **boring**.	While this could be true, most people do not say such a negative thing about themselves. A more typical meaning is that the person feels something.	I am very **bored**. This book is very **boring**. I am **bored** with **this boring book**.
☹ I dropped my cup of coffee on the floor in the hall. I was very **embarrassing**.	Other sets of such words include *embarrassed/ embarrassing*. The example sentence means that the person caused embarrassment for other people. Perhaps that was true. But, a more typical meaning would be about the emotion that the person felt.	I dropped my cup of coffee on the floor in the hall. I was very **embarrassed**. Learning a new language can be **embarrassing** because you make many mistakes. When I make a mistake in front of other people, I get **embarrassed**.

Choose the correct form in each sentence below.

1. Some students in my history class are <u>bored/boring</u>. They sleep through the teacher's lectures.

2. Some classes are <u>bored/boring</u>.

3. Listening to my economics professor is sometimes <u>interested/interesting</u> and sometimes <u>bored/boring</u>.

4. A three-hour lecture often makes me <u>tired/tiring</u>.

5. A three-hour lecture often is <u>tired/tiring</u> for me.

6. Getting a degree can be a <u>rewarded/rewarding</u> experience.

7. A <u>worked/working</u> student does not have much free time.

8. Visiting another college was an <u>interested/interesting</u> experience.

9. Failing a test is a <u>frustrated/frustrating</u> experience.

10. Many students are <u>disappointed/disappointing</u> with their final grades.

11. Even the students with the highest grades thought that the test yesterday was <u>frustrated/frustrating</u>.

12. After the test, even the best students in the class were <u>frustrated/frustrating</u>.

13. The last chapter in economics was <u>confused/confusing</u>.

14. I do not feel <u>relaxed/relaxing</u> in any of my classes.

15. Pizza has always had a <u>pleased/pleasing</u> aroma to me.

16. Some students are <u>fascinated/fascinating</u> by the computer.

17. For other students, computer sciences courses are not very <u>interested/interesting</u>.

18. I felt <u>rewarded/rewarding</u> for all my hard work after I received a Math Student of the Semester Award.

19. Several students were <u>surprised/surprising</u> when their math professor handed out a pop quiz yesterday.

20. Some students in my economics class are <u>confused/confusing</u>. They do not understand the professor's lectures.

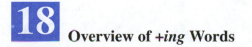

Other Units Related to This Topic

SECTION

VI

Numbers

Writing Numbers to Report Data and Factual Information

In your introductory composition courses, you will find that instructors usually expect you to follow the patterns given below. In more advanced courses, you will need to find out about the rules followed in particular fields of study. For example, in the social sciences, writers are often expected to follow the rules given in the *Publication Manual of the American Psychological Association.* In other fields of study, other methods for using numbers will be expected. Ask your instructors and your academic advisers about the publication manual that you are expected to use.

Numbers for Dates, Addresses, Chapters, Pages, Time, and Money

Use numerals to refer to dates, addresses, chapters, pages, time, and exact sums of money.

Days of the month	`January 1 is the first day of the year.`
	`Her birthday is June 22.`
Street addresses	`They live at 1019 Piedmont Ave.`
Chapter and page references	`The test will cover the information in Chapter 7.`
	`The homework exercises are on page 317.`

Time	Our class begins at **1:25 p.m.**
Exact sums of money	Student assistants are paid **$5.25 per hour.**

Numbers for Personal Information in Nontechnical Writing

Age. Write out the number in words for age. Use a hyphen to join two-word numbers.	My brother is **ten years old.** My sister is **fifteen.** My older brother is **twenty-five.**
Weight. If a weight can be given as a two-word number, use words. If a weight is a three-word number, use numerals.	My dog weighs **thirty-three** pounds. I weigh **153** pounds.
Height. Spell out heights in nontechnical writing.	She is **five feet tall.** She is **five feet two inches tall.**

Other Number Rules Often Used in Composition Courses

One to Ten. Numbers from one to ten are written as words rather than numbers if they do not represent precise measurements.	I go to the library **two or three** times each week.

Two-Word Round Numbers. Round numbers with no decimals are written as words when they have no more than two words. Generally, numbers that can be written in one or two words are given in words rather than in numbers.

Tickets to the baseball game cost **fifteen dollars** each.

This university is **one hundred years old.**

Exact Numbers. However, exact numbers are written as numerals. Exact numbers include exact counts, exact sums of money, technical measurements, decimals, fractions, and percentages.

This year, the university's enrollment is **26,211** students.

My apartment is **4.2 miles** from the university.

Percentages. Use numerals, but spell out the word *percent.*

Last quarter, **76 percent** of the students passed all of their courses.

Mixed Types in One Sentence. When a sentence involves both shorter and longer numbers, use numbers for all of them rather than mix the two different styles in one sentence.

In 1992, the university's enrollment was **22,379** students representing **45** U.S. states and **75** other countries.

Numbers at the Beginning of a Sentence. Avoid numerals at the beginning of sentences. Generally, writers can find some words to place in front of the numeral.

If the number can be written in words, it can come at the beginning of a sentence.

problem
☹ **26,211** students are registered at the university this fall.

revision
This fall, 26,211 students are registered at the university.

problem
☹ **20** students from my university went to Peru to study last summer.

revision
Twenty students from my university went to Peru to study last summer.

Punctuation for Numbers

Hyphens. When numbers 21–99 are spelled as words, a hyphen is used to connect the words: *twenty-one forty-six   ninety-nine*

Hyphens are also used for writing the words for fractions: *one-third two-sixths   four-sixteenths*

Tickets to the rock concert cost **twenty-five dollars** each.

My rent takes almost **one-third** of my income.

Colons. When times are written with a.m. or p.m., a colon is used to separate hours from minutes: *10:30 a.m 5:45 p.m.*

My calculus class is from **11:55 a.m. to 12:50 p.m.** on MWF.

Commas. In the U.S., a comma is used to separate the parts of large numbers. Other countries have different practices. Find out and use the appropriate standard: *1,120   10,000   100,000 1,000,000*

Atlanta has a population of more than **2,000,000.**

Periods. In the U.S., periods are used to mark decimals. Other countries have other practices. Find out and use the appropriate standard: *$120.50   6.12356*

My ticket to Tokyo cost **$1,250.33.**

 **Practice 1**

Correct the numbers in the following sentences.

1. Dr. Sylvia Krebs, a history professor at the University of Hawaii, has written 22 articles and 3 books about Latin American trade agreements.

2. 2 of her books and 15 of her articles are on reserve at the university library.

3. 1 article discusses the balance of trade and indicates that new trade agreements will raise exports by eleven percent.

19   **Writing Numbers**

4. By Monday, February sixteenth, every student must be prepared to present a 5-minute report on a topic discussed in the course.

5. 25 students out of the university's 25,000 students have the same assignment: prepare for the oral presentation and study Chapter Six.

☞ **Practice 2**

Correct the numbers in the following sentences.

1. 24 students answered the Teacher Evaluation Questionnaire; twenty would recommend the class, and 4 would not recommend it.

2. 15 thousand students completed the Student Opinion Survey last week.

3. The Student Opinion Survey is divided into 3 parts.

4. Most students prefer to attend classes between nine and one.

5. The average student must be fairly young because over seventy percent are under twenty-one.

Other Units Related to This Topic

✔ 9. Irregular Plural Nouns

✔10. Plural and Singular Forms: Consistency of Use in Writing

✔37. Commas

SECTION

VII

Parallelism

Grammatical and Logical Parallelism

Grammatical Parallelism

Grammatical parallelism is the result of coordination. When a coordinating conjunction is used to combine words, those words must be the same part of speech. The examples show parallelism when nouns, verbs, and adjectives are combined using coordinating conjunctions.

parallel nouns

```
In grammar class, we study
nouns, verbs, prepositions,
articles, and many other
topics.
```

parallel verbs

```
In grammar class, we read,
write, talk, and listen.
```

parallel adjectives

```
This class is difficult but
important.
```

118

Logical Parallelism

Combinations of words and phrases need to be grammatical, but they also need to involve parallel meaning. The items need to be of equal value and importance. Logical parallelism can be a major problem for writers if they do not think carefully about the items that are combined. In the second example, the writer chose words that we would not usually expect to be parallel but explained the choice.

This class is **difficult, interesting, and required** for all mathematics majors.

This class is both **difficult and easy.** It is difficult in that we have many assignments for homework and a 25-page research paper. It is easy because the content is familiar to me so that I am not struggling to learn new information.

Problems with Grammatical Parallelism

Problem 1

Not keeping the forms parallel in compound phrases

Problem	Solution	Revision
*My friend **took** my project and **copy** it.	The writer is describing past time events. Both verb forms should have the same simple past tense. Change *copy* to *copied.*	My friend **took** my project and **copied** it.
*In high school, our instructors **were** well educated and **known** how to handle their students.	The verb phrase should combine two simple past tense verbs. Change *known* to *knew.*	In high school, our instructors **were** well educated and **knew** how to handle their students.

*I **was** in many karate tournaments and **taken** a lot of first place awards.

The verb phrase should combine two simple past tense verbs. Change *taken* to *took*.

I **was** in many karate tournaments and **took** a lot of first place awards.

Problem 2

Omitting one of the number words from a series

Problem	Solution	Revision
☺Effective teachers must have these qualities. First, they must love teaching. Second, they must understand their subject. They must prepare carefully for every class.	The writer forgot to complete the series. Add the word *third* or some other counting word to make the passage parallel in structure.	Effective teachers must have these qualities. First, they must love teaching. Second, they must understand their subject. Third, they must prepare carefully for every class. Effective teachers must have these qualities. First, they must love teaching. Second, they must understand their subject. In addition, they must prepare carefully for every class.

Grammatical and Logical Parallelism

Problem

Putting unequals into a statement that suggests that they are of equal value or importance

Problem	Solution	Revision
☹ In the 21st century, the majority of the population in the United States will be African-American, Hispanic, Asian-American, and women.	The writer has a logical problem because the four groups listed are not of equal status: all the ethnic groups listed include women as well as men. Since women already make up approximately 51 percent of the United States population, they are already the majority. The writer needs to rethink his or her information to be more accurate in meaning.	In the United States in the 21st century, the population will have much higher percentages of African-Americans, Hispanics, and Asian-Americans. In the late 20th century, women are already over 50 percent of the population. Thus, in the 21st century, white males will not be in the majority in the population.

☛ **Practice 1**

Edit the following sentences to be sure that the verb phrases are parallel.

1. I believe that everyone has to study and learning about computers because they are required in all types of work and being used in all fields of study.

2. Without knowledge of computers, students cannot use the library efficiently or to use the computer lab to type their research papers.

3. Getting a doctoral degree requires many years of study and taken a lot of money.

4. Researchers have demonstrated that smoking is dangerous for one's health. Now it is time for people to recognize this information and reducing smoking cigarettes.

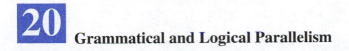

20 **Grammatical and Logical Parallelism** 121

5. To be successful in a job interview, we must look nice and to have a good attitude.

6. I want to get a good education and been a professional person.

7. The government can help people and to bring harm to people, too.

8. My parents have love and cared for me since my birth.

9. Without television, people in the U.S. could not visualize what happen and how it happens in other places around the world.

10. In high school, I saw other students cheat on their tests and on research papers because they wanted to got into better colleges and have better jobs.

☞ **Practice 2**

Topic sentences and thesis sentences frequently need parallel structures. Correct the parallelism mistakes in the following sentences. Some sentences already show correct parallelism.

1. We learn through our abilities to see, to hear, and to smell.

2. Dependability, determination, and most important self-disciplining are qualities that we expect a successful person to have.

3. If I earned $200,000 a year, my life would change emotionally, economically, and in my social activities.

4. In my opinion, war is not justified because people lose their lives, bad for foreign relationships, and economy.

5. People who know nothing about computers could find it difficult to find a job, hard to be promoted, and to earn enough money to send their children to college.

6. My friend said that I should smile more, and that advice has helped me in the United States to make more friends, had a better attitude, and became adjusted to life here.

7. Exercising frequently, choosing food carefully, and reduce daily stress are three ways that students can improve their lifestyle.

8. Self-discipline is an important ingredient for success; first, self-discipline gives a person a clear guideline for success; second, self-discipline makes a person's life more normal; third, most successful people have strong self-discipline.

9. Attending college in the United States has changed me; it has helped establish my confidence, offered me an opportunity to continue my education, and showed me that I can achieve my goals.

10. Students can gain knowledge at educational institutions, such as schools and colleges, and media—radio and television.

☞ Practice 3

Complete the following sentences using appropriate parallel structure.

1. The colors of the French flag are _____.

2. For breakfast, I like to eat _____.

3. Before I get to school, I do the following three things. First, _____ _____.

4. At our school, we have students from many different countries. For example, _____.

5. For exercise, I _____.

☞ Practice 4

The following paragraph is the first paragraph from a student essay. It has a problem with parallelism. Examine both the content and the language, and then improve the paragraph. For example, the long second sentence might be improved by breaking it into several sentences.

Punishment for Cheating

[1]Cheating, one of the most common crimes in college, should be penalized. [2]Tougher penalties like expulsion from college might stop potential cheaters; second, cheating hurts all students, and third, the most important reason, is that it will help eliminate bad habits and will help students develop moral and academic standards.

Other Units Related to This Topic

✔14. Coordinating Conjunctions

✔15. Compound Sentences

SECTION

VIII

Passive Sentences

21 Grammar and Use of Passive Sentences

Grammar and Use of Passive Sentences

The Grammar of Passive Sentences

Compare the grammar of these two sentences to review the differences between active and passive sentences.

active sentence

<u>The Chinese</u> <u>invented</u> paper money.

passive sentence

<u>Paper money</u> <u>was invented</u> by the Chinese.

Active vs. Passive Subject. The subject of a passive sentence receives the action of the verb. The subject of the active sentence does the action of the verb. Also, the subject of the passive sentence is the direct object of the active sentence.

active subject

the Chinese

active direct object

paper money

passive subject

paper money

Passive vs. Active Verb. The passive verb is formed by using the past participle of the active verb. The passive verb has this pattern: *be* + past participle of the verb.

active verb

invented

passive verb

was invented

***By*-Phrase 1.** The subject of the active sentence can be used in an adverbial phrase in the passive sentence. This phrase is called the *by-phrase*.

active subject

the Chinese

by-phrase

by the Chinese

By-Phrase 2. The *by*-phrase is not required. It should be used only when it provides important information. The *by*-phrase in the first example can easily be left out because only thieves "steal." In the second example, a more interesting *by*-phrase is used.

☹ My car was stolen last night by a thief.

My car was stolen last night by a twelve-year-old boy.

Using Passive Sentences

English speakers use passive sentences when they want to change the focus from the subject to the direct object of the verb. Passive sentences are used in the following situations.

Actor Unknown. For some events, it is impossible to know who did the action.

The wheel was invented early in the history of human civilization.

Actor Unimportant. The person who did the action is not the focus of the communication. For example, in technical and scientific writing, the focus is on the process rather than on the technician or the scientist. In other contexts, too, the focus can be on the events rather than on the people who were involved.

This report was prepared with a grant from the Ford Foundation.

This university was founded in 1889 to serve residents of this state.

Actor Hidden. The name of the actor can be left out of the communication to hide some information. This use of the passive can be interpreted positively or negatively based on differing points of view. John is probably grateful that his name is not mentioned. The boss probably needs to ask some questions.

John dropped the computer; Maria fixed it. Maria said to their boss: "The computer was damaged slightly when it was dropped, but I repaired it. Everything is fine now."

21 **Grammar and Use of Passive Sentences** · **127**

Choosing Between Active and Passive Versions of Sentences

Many verbs can have either an active or a passive form. The active form is used when the writer wants to focus on the actor or the actors. This writer is focusing on the students.

<u>All students at this school must take</u> English composition before they graduate. Many international students worry about this course because it is difficult for students who are not native speakers of English.

However, sometimes a writer wants to focus on the information that would be in the direct object in an active sentence. The passive sentence puts this information in the subject position. This writer is focusing on the English composition course.

<u>English composition must be taken</u> by all students at this school before they graduate. The course involves both argumentative and expository writing.

Passive Verb Forms

The passive verb can have all of the forms possible for the active verb.

The university's computers <u>are repaired</u> by the Computer Center.
My computer <u>is repaired</u> by my uncle.

Ten computers <u>were repaired</u> by the Computer Center this week.
My computer <u>was repaired</u> yesterday.

His computer <u>has been repaired</u> frequently.
My computer <u>had been repaired</u> before I bought it.

```
The computer is being
repaired.
The computer was being
repaired.

The computer has been being
repaired.
The computer had been being
repaired.

The computer will be
repaired.
The computer will have been
repaired.
The computer will be being
repaired.
The computer will have been
being repaired.
```

Problems with Passive Sentences

Problem 1

Not using the past participle

Problem	Solution	Revision
*English composition **must be take** by all students at this college.	Passive verbs use the past participle form of the main verb. Change *take* to *taken.*	English composition **must be taken** by all students at this college.
*Cheating is a serious problem. Students who cheat **must be punished** and **should not be allow** to continue in school.	The writer put two passive verbs together but did not use the correct verb for the second part. Add *+ed* to *allow* to make the past participle form of this regular verb.	Cheating is a serious problem. Students who cheat **must be punished** and **should not be allowed** to continue in school.

Problem 2

Confusing passive with present perfect verb forms

Problem	Solution	Revision
*By the end of the quarter, we **will be learned** more about American history.	*Learn* is seldom used as a passive verb. For the passive meaning, the verb *teach* is used. The writer has two choices for editing this sentence. The first example focuses on the students and their learning. The second example focuses on the students and their relationship with their teacher.	active verb = modal + perfect By the end of the quarter, we **will have learned** more about American history. passive verb = modal + perfect + passive By the end of the quarter, we **will have been taught** more about American history.
*Because of computers, typewriters **will be disappeared** in the twenty-first century.	For this meaning, *disappear* is an active verb. The writer is probably trying to use the perfect form with *have*.	Because of computers, typewriters **will have disappeared** in the twenty-first century.

Problem 3

Incorrect noun-pronoun agreement in the *by*-phrase

Problem	Solution	Revision
***Teachers** are evaluated by **his** students.	The writer has two choices to revise this sentence. (1) *Teachers* is a plural noun; change *his* to *their* for plural reference. (2) Make the subject singular, but remember that both men and women can be teachers. Change *his* to *her/his*.	**Teachers** are evaluated by **their** students. **A teacher** is evaluated by **her/his** students.

☞ Practice 1

Underline the passive verbs in the following sentences; then, make any necessary corrections. Identify the three sentences which should be written in active voice, not passive voice: (Sentence # ___, Sentence # ___ and Sentence # ___).

1. There are many differences between a technical school and a college: one difference is that a college is emphasized liberal arts subjects in addition to career subjects.

2. Once a student identifies his major and it listed on the college computer system, many course requirements are also identified.

3. Most introductory college courses are provided only general knowledge of the subject.

4. Many jobs today have something to do with computers because large amounts of data and information are store on computers.

5. When a person interviews for a job, it is important for that person to dress appropriately because applicants are often judge by the way that they dress.

6. Whispering in class while the teacher is lectured shows a lack of respect for the teacher and the other students in the class, and it is even worse for those who are sitting next to the student.

7. My brother, a fourth-year medical student, was catch cheating in his chemistry final exam; he failed that class.

8. A person's self-discipline and organization often depend on what was teached in childhood.

☞ Practice 2

Underline the passive verbs in the following sentences; then, make any necessary corrections.

1. Our knowledge can be improve by reading books and by making observations of the world around us.

2. When students study history, travel experiences can often remembered more easily than reading books.

3. Many students choose their major during their first year at college, but this decision is often change later.

4. Plagiarism should not be grounds for dismissal from college, but it should be punish.

Grammar and Use of Passive Sentences 131

5. Although many college students never go to see their academic advisors, choosing their own courses should not be allow because students often take courses that they really do not need.

6. College students dress in many different ways for many different reasons, and they should not be judge by the way that they dress.

7. A person who knows nothing about computers may not be hire as quickly as a person who has taken several computer courses at college.

8. I wish that my high-school grades and SAT scores could be change so that I could have gotten into a better college.

9. Developing good study habits is a very important quality to be acquire.

10. Some employers allow new employees to be trained on the job after they have been hire.

Other Units Related to This Topic

SECTION

IX

Subordination

UNIT 22

Complex Sentences and Sentence Combining

Complex Sentence Defined

Complex sentence is the name for a
particular type of sentence. A complex
sentence has at least two clauses: an
independent or main clause and a
dependent or subordinate clause.
Complex sentence is a useful term for
writers for two reasons. First, it is a
traditional term that will be used by
many teachers. Understanding the term
will improve communication with these
teachers. Second, complex sentences are
useful for writers because they provide
a tool for adding variety and exactness
to written English.

complex sentence with an adverbial clause

```
I had lived in England and
France before I moved to
Canada to study medicine.
```

complex sentence with relative clause

```
Students usually respect
teachers who prepare
carefully for class.
```

complex sentence with noun clause

```
Our teacher told us that we
must attend all classes to
make an "A" in this course.
```

Compound-Complex Sentence Defined

Compound-complex sentences are sometimes used in academic writing. These sentences are a combination of compound and complex sentences. A compound-complex sentence is a compound sentence with at least one dependent clause. The example sentence is a compound sentence with two dependent clauses.

compound-complex

I had lived in England
before I moved to Canada,
so I expected to understand
Canadians better than I do.

compound version (no dependent clauses)

I had lived in England, so
I expected to understand
Canadians.

Dealing with Prepositions in Complex Sentences

Complex sentences sometimes involve decisions about placement of a prepositional phrase. Compare the two versions of this complex sentence. In the more formal version, the preposition moves to the beginning of the dependent clause and the word *whom* is used. Both versions are made of two sentences; the second sentence is changed into a relative clause to use inside the first sentence.

1. The student sits next to
me in calculus class.
2. I borrowed these notes
from the student.

informal version

The student who I borrowed
these notes **from** sits next
to me in calculus class.

formal version

The student **from** whom I
borrowed these notes sits
next to me in calculus
class.

Sentence Combining

Sentence combining exercises usually ask you to combine two or more shorter sentences into one longer sentence.

Instructions: Combine the following sentences into one or two sentences.

```
1. People can benefit from
eating snack foods.
2. We often fall into the
habit of eating only snack
foods.
3. Sometimes these snack
foods even substitute for
regular meals.
```

These exercises give you practice at trying different sentence types. You can try coordination and subordination. You can also practice adding transitional words and phrases to make connections clearer between the sentences in the paragraph.

combination 1

```
Although people can benefit
from eating snack foods, we
often fall into the habit
of eating only these
snacks, and sometimes they
even substitute for regular
meals.
```

combination 2

```
People can benefit from
eating snack foods, but we
often fall into the habit
of eating only snack foods
and even substituting
snacks for regular meals.
```

combination 3

```
People can benefit from
eating snack foods.
However, we often fall into
the habit of eating only
these snack foods, and
sometimes they even
substitute for regular
meals.
```

Combine the following sentences into one paragraph with nine sentences.

Vietnamese

1. There are three major dialects of Vietnamese. Vietnamese is the official language of Vietnam.

2. This language is a tonal language like Chinese. This language has borrowed many words from Chinese.

3. China ruled Vietnam for a thousand years. Many Chinese words and phrases were introduced into the Vietnamese language.

4. In the seventeenth century, European missionaries developed a written language. This new language used the Latin alphabet.

5. Early in the twentieth century, Vietnamese scholars began to use this writing system. They called the new writing system *Quoc Ngu.*

6. *Quoc Ngu* uses the same alphabet as the English language. There are many differences between the languages.

7. *Quoc Ngu* does not change the verb form to show time differences. *Quoc Ngu* does not have irregular verbs.

8. The Vietnamese language and the English language do not have the same word order. *Quoc Ngu* does not place the adjective in front of the noun.

9. The Vietnamese language is different from the English language in verb forms. The Vietnamese language is different from the English language in word order.

Adapted from "Vietnam," *Collier's Encyclopedia.* 1987 ed.

☞ **Practice 2**

Analyze the sentence types in the following paragraph: sentences ___, ___, and ___ are simple; sentence ___ is compound; sentences ___, ___, ___, ___, ___, ___, and ___ are complex.

Working My Way Through College

¹There are many advantages of working and attending college at the same time. ²Now that I am a student at Iowa State University, I find that going to school and working at the same time have made my life more enjoyable for the following reasons. ³First, going to college is fun because I learn a lot about subjects that I am interested in and can make new friends that I can study with.

Complex Sentences and Sentence Combining   **137**

[4]This makes the subjects more understandable and more enjoyable. [5]For example, in my ESL 100 class, I met Jenny, who came from Hong Kong. [6]She and I have studied grammar together for two months, and studying together has made it easier for us to learn all the grammar rules. [7]Secondly, by working, I can make my life more enjoyable because I can earn extra money to pay my tuition and fees as well as make new friends at work. [8]Also, at work, I learn about responsibilities and practice my English. [9]I have also learned that earning money is hard work. [10]In summary, I believe that there are many advantages of attending school and working at the same time.[11]I have found that working and attending college is fun because it keeps me busy and because I can socialize with friends as well as learn to handle responsibility.

Other Units Related to This Topic

UNIT 23

Subordinating Conjunctions and Types of Subordination

Adverbial Clauses and Subordinating Words

Adverbial clauses function like single-word adverbs to give time, place, manner, reason, and other adverbial meanings.

adverbial clause of time
After we finished the examination, we were very tired.

adverbial clause of reason
Because we were very tired, we decided to go home rather than eat lunch with our friends.

The following words are used to make adverbial clauses. Notice that some of these words have other uses. For example, *as* can be a preposition, and *when* can be used to make relative clauses.

---

after	*even though*	*until*
although	*if*	*when*
as	*since*	*whenever*
as long as	*so that*	*wherever*
because	*unless*	*while*
before		

Noun Clauses and *That*

That can be used with certain verbs to create *noun clauses. That* connects a complete sentence to the verb. These noun clauses are the direct objects of the main verb.

> We think **that calculus is easier than philosophy.**
>
> Our teacher told us **that we would have a test next week.**

The following verbs often have noun clauses as their direct objects.

announce	*hope*	*suggest*
ask	*insist*	*tell*
assume	*know*	*think*
believe	*remind*	*wish*
conclude	*report*	*worry*
doubt	*say*	
feel	*state*	

Review of *Yes-No* and Information Questions

English has two major types of questions. *Yes-No Questions* usually call for a response of "yes" or "no." *Information Questions* are formed using *Question Words* such as *who, whom, what, when, where, why, which, how much,* and *how many.* Notice the position of the auxiliary verb in the examples. As the examples show, one of the differences between questions and sentences is word order. *Yes-No Questions* put an auxiliary in front of the subject. Information Questions put an auxiliary in front of the subject if the question word is not the subject of the question.

yes-no question

> Can you go to the library after class?

yes-no question

> Did you take calculus last fall?

information question: *who* is the subject of the question

> Who taught Physics 401 last year?

information question: *when* is the adverbial modifier of the question

> When will you take English 111?

information question: *who* is the direct object of the question—informal version

Who <u>should</u> <u>students</u> <u>ask</u> for advice about financial problems?

information question: *whom* is the direct object of the question—formal version

Whom <u>should</u> <u>students</u> <u>ask</u> for advice about financial problems?

Questions as Noun Clauses

When a question is placed inside a sentence as a clause, the word order is not like that in independent questions. The auxiliary is not placed in front of the subject. Forms of *do* are removed. Compare the independent question to the same question used as a clause.

<u>Will</u> <u>you</u> <u>take</u> calculus or physics?

Her question is whether <u>I</u> <u>will take</u> calculus or physics.

Whether <u>I</u> <u>will take</u> calculus or physics will be decided at registration.

<u>Do</u> <u>you</u> <u>speak</u> Arabic?

The teacher asked her if <u>she</u> <u>spoke</u> Arabic.

<u>Who</u> <u>will teach</u> Calculus 202?

The students want to know <u>who</u> <u>will teach</u> Calculus 202.

Who <u>can</u> <u>we</u> <u>ask</u> for information about the summer class schedule?

I wonder who <u>we</u> <u>can ask</u> for information about the summer class schedule.

Whom <u>can</u> <u>we</u> <u>ask</u> for information about the summer class schedule?

I wonder whom <u>we</u> <u>can ask</u> for information about the summer class schedule.

Where <u>do</u> <u>they</u> <u>live</u>?

I need to know where <u>they</u> <u>live</u>.

Why <u>did</u> <u>he</u> <u>cheat</u> on the test?

She cannot imagine why <u>he</u> <u>cheated</u> on the test.

Relative Clauses and Subordinating Words

A relative clause is also called *an adjective clause* because these clauses combine with nouns. They modify the meaning of a noun much as a regular adjective modifies the meaning of a noun.

relative clause modifying *the book*
I like the book **that you gave me for graduation.**

Two or more shorter sentences that share the same words can be combined into a complex sentence using relative clauses.

sentence 1
I like **the book.**

sentence 2
You gave me **the book** for graduation.

clause created from sentence 2
that you gave me for graduation

combination: sentence 1 with relative clause
I like **the book that you gave me for graduation.**

The following subordinating words are also called *relative pronouns*. They can be used to create relative clauses.

that	*where*	*who*	*whose*
when	*which*	*whom*	*why*

Restrictive vs. Nonrestrictive Relative Clauses

A *restrictive relative* clause provides information about its noun that "restricts" or "defines" the noun. In the example, the relative clause is used to identify the particular student being discussed.

`The student `**`who sits next`**
`to me in calculus`` missed`
`the final examination.`

A *nonrestricive relative clause* is one that is used with a noun that does not need additional information to "restrict" or "define" its meaning. When a nonrestrictive relative clause is used with a proper noun, as in the first example at right, the clause provides important information but is not needed to identify the person. A name is enough to identify the person being discussed. In the second example, there is only one president of the group, so the clause provides additional information that is not needed to identify the person. Notice the use of commas to separate the nonrestrictive relative clause from the rest of the sentence.

`Carlos Avalos, `**`who sits`**
`next to me in calculus,`
`missed the final`
`examination.`

`The president of our`
`student organization, `**`who`**
`comes from Venezuela,`
`organized a reception for`
`new students.`

Subordinating Conjunctions and Subordination   **143**

Restrictive Relative Clauses with Subject Pronouns: *Who*

Relative clauses can be used to combine two sentences that have the same subjects.

sentence 1

The professor comes from Korea.

sentence 2

The professor teaches my computer science class.

clause created from sentence 2

who teaches my computer science class

combination: sentence 1 with relative clause

The professor who teaches my computer science class comes from Korea.

In this example, the relative clause is added to the direct object of the first sentence.

sentence 1

At the reception for new students, I met **a Korean professor.**

sentence 2

The Korean professor teaches my computer science course.

clause created from sentence 2

who teaches my computer science course

combination: sentence 1 with relative clause

At the reception for new students, I met **the Korean professor who teaches my computer science course.**

Restrictive Relative Clauses with Subject Pronouns: *That*

That is used when the relative clause refers to something other than a human being.

sentence 1

I need **information.**

sentence 2

The information explains the transportation system in London.

clause created from sentence 2

that explains the transportation system in London

combination: sentence 1 with relative clause

I need **information that explains the transportation system in London.**

That can also be used to refer to human beings. However, some composition teachers do not like this use for formal written English. Some teachers prefer the use of *who*. It is generally wise to follow the preferences of your teachers.

sentence 1

At the reception for new students, I met **the professor.**

sentence 2

The professor will teach my calculus class.

combination with *that*

At the reception for new students, I met **the professor that will teach my calculus class.**

combination with *who*

At the reception for new students, I met **the professor who will teach my calculus class.**

Subordinating Conjunctions and Subordination

Restrictive Relative Clauses with Object Pronouns: *Whom*

In these examples, two sentences have the same direct object. A new sentence is made by turning one of the sentences into a relative clause. Notice that the formal version requires *whom*, but that *who* is possible in informal communication.

sentence 1

At the reception for new students, I met **a professor.**

sentence 2

You have **the professor** for your English class.

clause created from sentence 2: formal version

whom you have for your English class

clause created from sentence 2: less formal version

who you have for your English class

combination: formal version

At the reception for new students, I met **the professor whom you have for your English class.**

combination: less formal version

At the reception for new students, I met **the professor who you have for your English class.**

23

Restrictive Relative Clauses and Objects of Prepositions: *Whom*

Relative clauses can also be formed that involve the objects of prepositions. Notice the differences between the formal and the less formal versions. One problem that some writers have with the less formal version is forgetting to include the preposition.

sentence 1

At the reception for new students, I met **the student.**

sentence 2

My roommate bought his car **from the student.**

clause created from sentence 2: formal version

from whom my roommate bought his car

clauses created from sentence 2: less formal version

whom my roommate bought his car from
who my roommate bought his car from

combination: formal version

At the reception for new students, I met **the student from whom my roommate bought his car.**

combinaton: less formal version

At the reception for new students, I met **the student whom my roommate bought his car from.**

combination: less formal version

At the reception for new students, I met **the student who my roommate bought his car from.**

problem: leaving out the preposition

*At the reception for new students, I met the student who my roommate bought his car.

23 **Subordinating Conjunctions and Subordination** 147

Restrictive Relative Clauses with Object Pronouns: *That*

In these examples, the subject of one sentence has the same information as the direct object of the second sentence.

sentence 1

The textbook costs $59.

sentence 2

Dr. Stokes will require **the textbook** next quarter.

clause created from sentence 2

that Dr. Stokes will require next quarter

combination: sentence 1 with relative clause

The textbook that Dr. Stokes will require next quarter costs $59.

Restrictive Relative Clauses with *Whose*

Whose is used to replace a possessive noun to make relative clauses like the one in this example.

sentence 1

At the reception for new students, I met **the professor.**

sentence 2

The professor's textbook is required for our biology class.

clause created from sentence 2

whose textbook is required for our biology class

combination: sentence 1 with relative clause

At the reception for new students, I met **the professor whose textbook is required for our biology class.**

Omitting the Relative Pronoun

The relative pronoun can be omitted if it is not the subject of the relative clause. *That* is the direct object of the relative clause formed from this sentence: *Dr. Stokes will require the textbook next quarter.*

relative pronoun included

The textbook <u>that</u> Dr. Stokes will require next quarter costs $59.

relative pronoun omitted: direct object of relative clause

The textbook Dr. Stokes will require next quarter costs $59.

These examples show omission of the relative pronoun from other types of relative clauses. All of these examples are taken from the explanations given previously.

relative pronoun omitted: object of preposition

At the reception for new students, I met **the student my roommate bought his car from.**

relative pronoun omitted: direct object

At the reception for new students, I met **the professor you have for your English class.**

If the relative pronoun is the object of a preposition and if the formal version is used so that the preposition is moved to the beginning of the relative clause, then the relative pronoun cannot be omitted.

problem: relative pronoun cannot be omitted

*At the reception for new students, I met **the student from my roommate bought his car.**

revision: relative pronoun added after the preposition

At the reception for new students, I met **the student from whom my roommate bought his car.**

Subordinating Conjunctions and Subordination   **149**

If the relative pronoun is the subject of the relative clause, it cannot be omitted.

problem: subject of the relative clause is missing

*At the reception for new students, I met **the professor will teach my calculus class.**

revision: *who* is added as the subject for the relative clause

At the reception for new students, I met **the professor who will teach my calculus class.**

The Many Uses of *That*

Relative Clauses. The word *that* is used for relative clauses. In this example, *that* replaces the direct object of sentence 2. *That* means "the two textbooks."

that in a relative clause

I bought the two textbooks **that our teacher required for Biology 301.**

sentence 1

I bought **the two textbooks.**

sentence 2

Our teacher required **the two textbooks** for Biology 301.

clause created from sentence 2

that our teacher required for Biology 301

Noun Clauses. *That* is used with certain verbs to attach noun clauses as direct objects of the sentence.

that in a noun clause

Our biology teacher said **that we had to buy two expensive textbooks.**

Noun Clauses. *That* is used in noun clauses created from a verb + *that* + clause. These look like relative clauses but have different grammar; *that* is simply a connecting word and is not a grammatical part of the clause.

noun clause: verb + *that* + clause

I believe **that textbooks are too expensive.**

noun clause: verb changed to noun form + *that* + clause

My belief that textbooks are too expensive is shared by many students.

Determiner. Also, *that* can be used as a determiner. In this use, *that* is also often called a demonstrative pronoun.

that as a determiner

The textbooks for **that biology course** were expensive.

Coordinating Conjunctions and Subordinating Conjunctions with Similar Meanings

But and *although* are similar in meaning. They are used in different ways. Notice the difference in their punctuation.

I wanted to study the piano, **but** my family could not afford the lessons.

Although I wanted to study the piano, my family could not afford the lessons.

For and *because* are similar in meaning. However, *for,* in this sense, is seldom used and is limited to very formal contexts.

We were surprised by the length of the test, **for** we had expected only a short one for the mid-term exam.

We were surprised by the length of the test **because** we had expected only a short one for the mid-term exam.

Problems with Complex Sentences and Subordinate Clauses

Problem 1

Creating a fragment by using a subordinate clause as an independent clause

Problem	Solution	Revision
Smoking in public places can cause health problems. *Because people are trapped in rooms with the smoke.	The writer needs to combine the *because*-clause with the first part of the sentence to make a complex sentence. In speaking, we often pause before such clauses, but in writing they must be combined with an independent clause to make a complex sentence. Notice that the combination is made by removing the period and using a lower case letter; no comma is used.	Smoking in public places can cause health problems because people are trapped in rooms with the smoke.

Problem 2

Using *that* rather than *which* in a nonrestrictive relative clause

Problem	Solution	Revision
*The Mona Lisa, that Leonardo Da Vinci painted in 1504, can be seen at the Louvre in Paris.	*That* is used for restrictive relative clauses. When using nonrestrictive relative clauses to give information about identified nouns, use *which* for things and *who* or *whom* for people.	The Mona Lisa, which Leonardo Da Vinci painted in 1504, can be seen at the Louvre in Paris.

Using the wrong word order when a question becomes a dependent clause

Problem	Solution	Revision
*My teacher asked me why did I miss the test.	The writer has the correct word order for a question: *why did you miss the test?* However, when the question is used as a dependent clause, the word order changes back to basic sentence order. Remove *did.* Change *miss* to *missed.*	My teacher asked me why I missed the test.

Problem 4

Omitting a required preposition from a relative clause

Problem	Solution	Revision
*I want to take only courses that count my major.	The writer is trying to combine these sentences: 1. *I want to take courses.* 2. *The courses count for my major.* The preposition *for* is missing from the relative clause. The clause should be *that count for my major.*	I want to take only courses that count for my major.

Subordinating Conjunctions and Subordination   153

*In the library, I can find many books that I can get information for my research project.

The writer is trying to combine these sentences:

1. *In the library, I can find many books.*
2. *I can get information from the books for my research project.*

The preposition *from* is missing from the relative clause. The clause should be *that I can get information from for my research project.*

In the library, I can find many books that I can get information from for my research project.

Not forming the relative clause correctly

Problem	Solution	Revision
*The newspaper that I read it every day has excellent international coverage.	The writer is trying to combine these sentences: 1. *The newspaper has excellent international coverage.* 2. *I read the newspaper every day.* The relative clause should be *that I read every day.* In English, the relative pronoun has two jobs: (1) it replaces a word in the clause, and (2) it connects the clause to the noun. In some languages, the relative pronoun is just a connecting word, so some writers have this problem because they add an unnecessary extra pronoun. Remove *it.*	The newspaper that I read every day has excellent international coverage.

☞ Practice 1

Add words to complete the relative clauses in the following sentences.

1. We live in a society that _____.

2. A student is a person who _____.

3. Cigarette smokers ignore the danger that _____.

4. A dictionary is a book that _____.

5. A teacher is a person whom _____.

☞ Practice 2

Add words to complete the following clauses.

1. I think that in the future _____.

2. I believe that _____.

3. It is true that _____.

4. I am sure that _____.

5. In my family, we agree that _____.

6. My teacher asked me why _____.

7. To get to his apartment for the party, Carlos explained where _____.

☞ Practice 3

In this exercise, find and correct the problems. One of these sentences is correct.

1. The books that I must buy them for my classes are very expensive.

2. I thought that learning English would be easy. Because I would live in the United States.

3. The best advice that I ever received it was to have self-discipline in my work.

4. Although I studied hard. I did not receive the best grade in the class.

5. I was unhappy because of many things bothered me about the demands that my parents made for me to make only As.

6. These are the questions that all people ask themselves about life.

7. I like the teachers I get an "A" for my final grade.

Subordinating Conjunctions and Subordination   **155**

8. I feel strongly that parents must guide the lives of their children. Because children do not understand many of the dangerous aspects of life.

9. I learned many lessons from my mother and father. When I was growing up in my home country.

10. Being good communicators in who people can believe is important for all political leaders.

☞ Practice 4

Combine the following sentences into one paragraph with nine sentences. Use subordination.

The Languages of India

1. The people of India speak 14 major languages. The major languages include more than 1,000 minor languages and dialects.

2. The major languages of India belong to two language families. One family is Indo-European. One family is Dravidian.

3. The Indo-European languages are spoken by about 75 percent of the people. These people live mainly in the northern and central regions.

4. They include Hindi and Urdu. Urdu is closely related to Hindi.

5. These languages come from Sanskrit. Sanskrit is an ancient Indian language. Sanskrit has many words similar to words in European languages.

6. Dravidian languages are spoken by about 24 percent of the people. These people live in the southern part of India.

7. Hindi is the official language of India. Hindi is the native language of about a third of the people.

8. India's Constitution of 1950 identified Hindi as the official language. India's Constitution of 1950 identified English as the language for government and business.

9. Generally, Indians live in the same state. Indians speak the same language.

Adapted from "India," *World Book Encyclopedia.* 1988 ed.

☞ Practice 5

Combine the following sentences by turning the second sentence into a relative clause in the first sentence.

1. Pepe has a friend. The friend's family lives in Paris.

2. The student speaks five languages. The student's family lives in Paris.

3. Maria knows a student. The student's backpack was stolen from the library last week.

4. The student was very angry because her textbooks were in the backpack. The student's backpack was stolen in the library.

5. Alexios bought a book. The book's author lives in Mexico.

6. The book won an international award. The book's author lives in Mexico.

☞ Practice 6

Analyze the subordinate clauses in the following paragraph. There are _____ adverb clauses, _____ relative clauses, and _____ noun clauses.

Working My Way Through College

[1]There are many advantages of working and attending college at the same time. [2]Now that I am a student at Iowa State University, I find that going to school and working at the same time have made my life more enjoyable for the following reasons. [3]First, going to college is fun because I learn a lot about subjects that I am interested in and can make new friends that I can study with. [4]This makes the subject more understandable and more enjoyable. [5]For example, in my ESL 100 class, I met Jenny, who came from Hong Kong. [6]She and I have studied grammar together for two months, and studying together has made it easier for us to learn all the grammar rules. [7]Secondly, by working, I can make my life more enjoyable because I can earn extra money to pay my tuition and fees as well as make new friends at work. [8]Also, at work, I learn about responsibilities and practice my English. [9]I have also learned that earning money is hard work. [10]In summary, I believe that there are many advantages of attending school and working at the same time. [11]I have found that working and attending college is fun because it keeps me busy and because I can socialize with friends as well as learn to handle responsibility.

Subordinating Conjunctions and Subordination   **157**

☞ **Practice 7**

Analyze the subordinate clauses in the following paragraph. There are _____ relative clauses, _____ noun clauses, and _____ adverb clauses.

My Favorite Season of the Year

[1]My favorite season of the year is winter because I like snow and winter sports. [2]When I was a young boy, I always liked to play in the snow. [3]Today, when I see snow on the ground, I think about my childhood and the good times that I had with my friends and my family. [4]In addition, when snow covers the ground, the world looks pure white and fresh. [5]I also like winter because skiing is one of my favorite sports. [6]Even though I have never tried to ski, I like to watch the competitions on television. [7]When I see the Olympic Ski Competition on television, I like to look at the snow on the mountains, but mostly I like to watch the athletes. [8]I also like ice hockey and believe that it is the best sport in the world. [9]Actually, when I was young, I was an amateur ice hockey player, so I know the skill that is required to play the game well. [10]I believe that ice hockey is one of the fastest sports in the world and requires players to think quickly. [11]Although I love snow and winter sports, I can't enjoy the winter season now because I live in Miami, Florida. [12]However, when I move to the Northwest, I will once again be able to enjoy the winter season.

Other Units Related to This Topic

✔**14.** Coordinating Conjunctions

✔**22.** Complex Sentences and Sentence Combining

✔**24.** Making Transitions and Using Transition Words

✔**37.** Commas

✔**40.** Fragments

✔**42.** Semicolons

SECTION

X

Transition

Making Transitions and Using Transition Words

Transition Words and Expressions

Transition words and expressions show the relationship between ideas within a sentence or between sentences. They are added to make sure that the reader understands the relationship that the writer wants to express. In the first example, the writer assumes that the reader will understand the relationship between the two sentences. In the second version of these sentences, the writer adds a transition word to be sure that the meaning is clear.

I can understand the fears of failure that cause some students to cheat on tests. I do not think that their fears are an excuse for criminal behavior.

I can understand the fears of failure that cause some students to cheat on tests. **However,** I do not think that their fears are an excuse for criminal behavior.

Many of these words and expressions are set off by commas. Notice the difference between the punctuation of the transition word depending on its location in the sentence.

transition expression at the beginning of a sentence
Many people like to stay up late at night. **As a result,** they do not like to take classes early in the morning.

transition word at the beginning of a sentence
I stay up late every night. **However,** I still prefer early classes so that I can play tennis in the afternoon.

160

Many students like to stay up late at night and, **as a result,** do not like to take classes early in the morning.

I stay up late every night; **however,** I still prefer early classes.

Coordinating Conjunctions and Subordinating Conjunctions with Meanings Similar to Transition Words and Phrases

Conjunction	Transition Words	Example
For. The coordinating conjunction *for* is seldom used. The subordinating conjunction *because* is more common. Other possibilities include transition words and phrases that refer to reasons and results.	*as a result* *consequently* *then* *therefore*	I am majoring in biology, **for** I want to be a medical doctor. I want to be a medical doctor; **therefore,** I am majoring in biology. I did not understand the assignment; **as a result,** I made a very low grade.

And. This coordinating conjunction has many meanings. Transition words can be added to make the meaning more exact. Or, transition words can be substituted. Be careful to select a word with the correct meaning.

also
furthermore
in addition

English 111 is required for all students, **and** they must take Biology 101, too.

English 111 is required for all students; **also,** they must take Biology 101.

English 111 is required for all students; **in addition,** they must take Biology 101.

Nor. The coordinating conjunction is used for "negative" choices. Substitution of a transition word will usually require major revision of the sentence to be sure the meaning remains the same.

furthermore
in addition

Smoking is not allowed in classrooms, **nor** can we smoke in the cafeteria.

Smoking is not allowed in classrooms; **furthermore,** we cannot smoke in the cafeteria.

But. This coordinating conjunction is used to set up contrasts. It is important to use the correct punctuation when using *however* and other substitutes for coordinating conjunctions. Subordinating conjunctions such as *although* can also be used as a substitute for *but.*

however
instead
nevertheless

Knowledge of computers is not required for graduation, **but** I think that all students should be computer literate.

Knowledge of computers is not required for graduation; **nevertheless,** I think that all students should be computer literate.

Although knowledge of computers is not required for graduation, I think that all students should be computer literate.

Or. This coordinating conjunction sets up choices. If only one of the choices is possible, the meaning is similar to *but.* If both choices are possible, the meaning is similar to *and.* The example means that students must make a choice between two times of day for the class.

also
in addition
too
if not
on the other hand

We can take English 111 in the morning, **or** we can wait until late in the afternoon for this class.

We can take English 111 in the morning; **on the other hand,** we can wait until late in the afternoon for this class.

24   **Making Transitions and Using Transition Words**

Yet. Generally, this coordinating conjunction is used to make a comment on something that was previously stated. *But* is a more frequently used word.	*however* *nevertheless* *still*	My roommate studies very hard, **yet** he cannot do well on tests. My roommate studies very hard, **but** he cannot do well on tests. My roommate studies very hard; **still,** he cannot do well on tests.
So. This coordinating conjunction is frequently used to give consequences. The subordinating conjunction *because* can be substituted.	*as a result* *consequently* *for this reason* *therefore*	Computers are used in all areas of modern life, **so** college graduates need to be computer literate. College graduates need to be computer literate **because** computers are used in all areas of modern life. Computers are used in all areas of modern life; **for this reason,** college graduates need to be computer literate.

After, before, when, while, **and other time words.** Writers can vary their sentences by using transition words rather than these subordinating conjunctions. Be careful to use correct punctuation.	*first, second,* etc. *next* *then*	I will enter medical school **after** I get a bachelor's degree in biology. **First,** I will get a bachelor's degree in biology. **Then,** I will enter medical school.	

Formality Levels for Transition Words and Expressions

Meaning	Basic Form for Informal and Formal Use	More Formal	Most Formal
ADDITION	*also* *first, second,* etc.	*additionally* *besides* *further* *furthermore* *in addition* *last but not least* *next* *not only . . . but* *also* *too*	*equally important* *moreover* *similarly*
CAUSE-EFFECT	*then* *therefore*	*as a result* *for this reason* *thus*	*accordingly* *as a consequence* *consequently* *hence*

Meaning	Basic Form for Informal and Formal Use	More Formal	Most Formal
COMPARISON	*also* *like* *too*	*as well as* *both . . . and* *compared to* *in the same way* *likewise* *neither. . . nor*	*by comparison* *in common with* *similarly* *in like manner*
CONTRAST	*however*	*instead* *nevertheless* *on the other hand*	*conversely* *in contrast to* *in opposition to* *on the contrary* *otherwise* *still* *whereas*
EXAMPLE	*for example*	*for instance* *in other words*	*as an example* *as an illustration* *to exemplify*
SUMMARY—CONCLUSION	*finally* *therefore*	*after all* *all in all* *at last* *briefly* *consequently* *last* *on the whole* *thus*	*accordingly* *as a consequence* *in brief* *in closing* *in conclusion* *in short* *in sum* *in summary* *to conclude* *to summarize*

Meaning	Basic Form for Informal and Formal Use	More Formal	Most Formal
TIME	*after a while* *after that* *also* *at last* *currently* *earlier* *eventually* *finally* *first, second*, etc. *in the future* *in the past* *last* *next* *now*	*afterward* *at the same time* *formerly* *immediately* *in the meantime* *later*	*concurrently* *previously* *simultaneously* *subsequently*

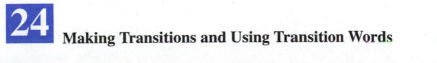

Problem 1

Using excessive numbers of transition words in a paragraph

Problem	Solution	Revision
☹A good mother must not have only love for her children but also determination to help them in all areas. **For example,** a supportive mother will not let her children starve. **In other words,** she will do whatever she has to do to find food for her children. **In addition,** she makes sure that her children have clothes to wear and a place to sleep. **Moreover,** a supportive mother will nurture her children both physically and psychologically. **As a result,** her children will always know that they can go to their mother for advice and help.	In academic writing, generally writers use a limited number of transition words in a paragraph. Transition words are used when the writer is concerned about the clarity of the relationship between two sentences. As a general rule, try to limit yourself to one or two transition words for every 150–200 words. The writer has used five transition phrases in a very short paragraph. In editing this paragraph, the writer needs to reduce the transition words to those that are most important to emphasize her/his meaning. The revision shows one way the paragraph could be changed. This revision assumes that the reader will understand that the writer is giving examples. The transition words are reserved to emphasize the results that the writer sees coming from a mother's love and devotion to her children.	A good mother must not have only love for her children but also determination to help them in all areas. A supportive mother will not let her children starve. She will do whatever she has to do to find food for her children. She makes sure that her children have clothes to wear and a place to sleep. A supportive mother will nurture her children both physically and psychologically. **As a result,** her children will always know that they can go to their mother for advice and help.

Problem 2

Using transition words that are not commonly used in academic writing

Problem	Solution	Revision
☹ **Nowadays** life in cities is like living in a jungle.	*Nowadays* is considered somewhat old-fashioned and is unlikely to be used by many native speakers in their written English. *Nowadays* and *now days* are used more in speaking than in writing. Writers are more likely to use a word such as *currently* or *these days*.	**In the late twentieth century,** life in cities is like living in a jungle.

Problem 3

Using coordinating conjunctions at the beginning of a sentence

Problem	Solution	Revision
☹ I want to obtain a good education. And I want to get a good job that pays well and has a lot of opportunities for promotion.	Many teachers and writers do not like the use of a coordinating conjunction at the beginning of a sentence. They prefer a transition word in that position. They reserve coordinating conjunctions for use in making compound sentences. It is generally wise to use the style preferred by your instructors.	transition word between two separate sentences I want to obtain a good education. Also, I want to get a good job that pays well and has a lot of opportunities for promotion. compound sentence I want to obtain a good education, and I want to get a good job that pays well and has a lot of opportunities for promotion.

Using transition words as if they were coordinating conjunctions—creating comma splices

Problem	Solution	Revision
★I know how to type, however, my speed is very slow.	Only the FANBOYS words can be used to create compound sentences using commas. FANBOYS is a reminder that the coordinating conjunctions are *for, and, nor, but, or, yet,* and *so.* The writer has created a problem called a comma splice. It can be corrected in several ways that are illustrated in the "Comma Splice" unit of this book. The revision shows three ways to correct this problem.	I know how to type. **However,** my speed is very slow. I know how to type; **however,** my speed is very slow. I know how to type, **but** my speed is very slow.
	(1) Change the comma after *type* to a period, and use a capital *H.* (2) Change the comma after *type* to a semicolon. (3) Use the coordinating conjunction *but* rather than the transition word *however.*	

One of the following sentences is correct; edit the sentences that have errors. Revisions can be made using changes in punctuation and word choice.

1. At home in China, I learned English pronunciation and vocabulary from the radio, therefore the radio can be a source of education.

2. Children do not have much experience or knowledge as a result parents must guide them carefully.

3. When my roommate got angry, I apologized however he did not accept my apology and he tried to make me find another place to live.

4. People have many different opinions on everything; thus, effective leaders have to know how to listen to people with whom they disagree.

5. It is not common for a four-year-old child to learn to ski, however, my parents let me take lessons because I wanted to so much, and now I am on the university's ski team and have a scholarship that pays my tuition.

☞ **Practice 2**

Replace the coordinating conjunction in each of the following sentences with a transition word of similar meaning. Be sure to edit for correct punctuation after the change. Some long sentences might be rewritten as two or more shorter sentences.

1. Computers can increase productivity, so even small companies need to consider computerization.

2. More and more companies are establishing non-smoking areas, and they are hiring non-smokers.

3. My family is not rich, and I am a college student, so I have to work to pay my tuition.

4. In Korean culture, the oldest son has to take care of his parents, and I am the oldest son, so I know that I will have responsibility for my parents when they are old.

5. If I won the lottery, my current life would change, but more importantly my future would change, too.

☞ **Practice 3**

The writer of this paragraph has used excessive numbers of transition words and phrases. Decide which words to remove. Decide which transition words or phrases must be kept for the meaning to remain clear.

Conclusion to an Essay on Sources of Knowledge

[1]In conclusion, television and personal experience can be valuable sources of knowledge. [2]However, they should be used in a meaningful and efficient manner. [3]Thus, you cannot just watch television but must choose shows carefully. [4]In addition, not all personal experience will increase knowledge. [5]And, you should not think that formal education is to be replaced by informal education. [6]Most importantly, you should remember that being knowledgeable often leads to success and satisfaction.

Other Units Related to This Topic

✔**14.** Coordinating Conjunctions

✔**15.** Compound Sentences

✔**22.** Complex Sentences and Sentence Combining

✔**23.** Subordinating Conjunctions and Types of Subordination

SECTION

XI

Verbs

Future Time Writing

Verb Choices for Future Time Meaning

English provides writers with many choices for communication about future time. In addition to various choices for verbs, writers can also indicate future time with adverbs and time phrases.

Choice 1. All *modal auxiliaries* can be used for future time meanings. In addition to indicating future time, they also have other meanings that are explained in the "Modal Auxiliary Verb" unit of this book. *Will* is the most frequently used modal for future time. *Will* also indicates that the writer is very convinced of the certainty of the statement.

future time promise/certainty

I **will meet** you at the cafeteria at 1:00 p.m.

future time slight probability

We **might go** to the cafeteria before we go to the library.

Choice 2. Simple present tense verbs can be used for scheduled events in the future. The verbs most often used include *arrive, be, begin, close, end, leave, open,* and *start.*

Our flight to Boston **leaves** at 2:15 p.m. this afternoon.

Choice 3. Present progressive verbs are used for communication about scheduled future time events. An adverbial of time is usually included to clarify the future time meaning.

Our flight to Boston **is leaving** at 2:15 p.m. this afternoon.

Choice 4. *Be going to* + verb is used to communicate about things that have been planned. *Be going to* + verb means that the future time events are the result of some current time plan. However, *will* has a strong meaning of "promise" or "certainty" and is generally limited to sentences of future time promise or determination. *Be going to* + verb is used for future time plans but without the emotional overtones of promise/determination that are

associated with *will*. *Be going to* + verb is frequently used in conversations but is also used in writing.

```
I am going to go to the
library after class.
```

Choice 5. Simple present tense verbs are used in dependent clauses when the main clause refers to future time, especially when a modal is used in the main clause.

```
We will go to the library
after we eat lunch.

I am going to eat lunch in
the cafeteria before I go
to the library.
```

Writing Conclusions

Some writers find conclusions especially difficult to write. One effective technique is to write predictions of future results of the materials presented in the body of the paper. These paragraphs are the conclusions for two essays that discuss whether or not the United States should restrict the import of foreign cars. While the writers completely disagree with each other, they both use the same technique to come to a conclusion.

Conclusion to Essay 1

```
More and more foreign cars
are imported into the United
States every year. This is
bad for the future of the
country. The United States
should severely restrict
the importation of foreign
cars for sale in America
because it will put the
American people back to
work. This change in policy
will also help the future
generations of the country
by having them grow up in a
stronger, more productive
economy.
```

Future Time Writing

```
In the United States, people
can enjoy luxury, fuel
economy, and fewer expenses
at the same time if they
buy a fine Japanese car.
Therefore, the United
States government should
reduce restrictions on
imported cars so that
American consumers will
have even greater
opportunities for
outstanding car values.
```

☞ **Practice 1**

Examine the use of future time in the following paragraph by marking all verbs and time markers. How many different ways of indicating future time are used by this writer?

Benefits of My College Education

[1]I expect my college education is going to change the rest of my life. [2]Without an education, finding a good job will be difficult. [3]Only an education will give me the kind of career that I want, and if I work toward my goal, I expect to get the results that I deserve.

☞ **Practice 2**

Underline the future time verbs and markers in the following essay. Notice the choices made by the writer. Make five changes in verbs below.

The Impact of My College Education

[1]I expect my college education to have a profound impact on the rest of my life. [2]I believe that the person I will be after graduating from college would be distinctly different from the person I was when I entered college.

[3]Leaving the protection of my family and country to attend college here in the United States has given me a sense of independence. [4]I have had to develop survival skills and become responsible because I am now accountable for all of my actions. [5]This new independence affects my future because I would not feel the need to depend on other people.

Future Time Writing 25

⁶At college, I met a variety of people from different countries, races, backgrounds, and religions. ⁷This has made me tolerant of other people and also open-minded and willing to learn about other cultures. ⁸This would affect the rest of my life because I would look for similarities in people instead of differences. ⁹I will also raise my children to be tolerant of other people.

¹⁰Because of my experiences at college, I am also able to work well with other people. ¹¹I have developed self-discipline and am able to meet deadlines. ¹²I have also become efficient and punctual. ¹³These are traits that I believe will be needed to obtain a job and to survive in the workplace. ¹⁴Thus, I will be more capable of acquiring a job and keeping it.

¹⁵My college education will make me more independent, self-disciplined, open-minded, and knowledgeable. ¹⁶These traits would change the rest of my life by making me more capable of co-existing with other people in society and also by making me a more desirable employee. ¹⁷My college education is going to change the rest of my life by making me a leader rather than a follower.

Other Units Related to This Topic

✔23.   Subordinating Conjunctions and Types of Subordination

✔26.   General Truth and Generalizations: Present Tense

✔28.   Modal Auxiliary Verbs

26

General Truth and Generalizations: Present Tense

Using Simple Present Tense Verbs

Choice 1. Simple present tense verbs can be used to mean **future time for a scheduled event.**

Our flight **leaves** at 2:15 p.m. this afternoon.

Choice 2. Simple present tense verbs are used in a **subordinate clause when the main verb is about future time.**

After we **arrive** in Montreal, we **will visit** with our friends before we all **go** to a baseball game together.

Choice 3. Simple present tense is used with **stative verbs for present time meaning.** These verbs cannot usually be used in the progressive verb form. See the "Present Time" unit of this book for more information.

I **feel** really good because I passed the test.

This soup **tastes** just like the kind my mother makes.

Ali **loves** chemistry and hates philosophy.

Choice 4. Generalizations are usually made using simple present tense forms of verbs. This use is especially important in academic writing.

This city **needs** improved public transportation.

Pollution **threatens** everyone's health.

General Truth Meaning

Generalizations can be made about personal habits.

I **play** tennis every Friday afternoon.

Maria **studies** in the library.

Jorge **works** in the physics laboratory.

Generalizations are also made about non-personal information, including scientific and technical information.

Water **consists** primarily of hydrogen and oxygen with traces of other substances.

Grammatical Features of Generalizations

Usually the verb will be simple present tense.

Holidays **give** people opportunities to celebrate, but they also **provide** rest and **help** us feel that we **are** part of a larger group of people with similar interests.

Sometimes the verb phrase includes *will* or another modal auxiliary to indicate the writer's degree of certainty about the facts. These examples are not about future time.

Oil **will not mix** with water.

During winter in Alaska, the sun **will shine** only for a limited time each day. People **must live** their daily lives in the dark.

In generalizations, nouns are usually in one of the generic forms. This means that certain choices of *a/an* or *the* must be used to indicate that classes or groups are being discussed. Notice the use of noncount nouns for generic meaning in the first example: *life* and *water*. The first example also uses plural nouns without articles for generic meaning: *environments, plants,* and *animals.* The second example includes several different types of generic nouns: *the elephant* refers to all elephants as a group. *Lions* and *monkeys* are plural forms without articles that refer to classes of animals rather than particular animals. *An African* and *an American* mean "typical members of these groups" and not particular people.

Life depends on adequate amounts of **water**. However, adequate has different meanings in different **environments**. Desert **plants** and **animals** require less **water** than most other forms of life.

The elephant lives in Asia and in Africa. **Lions, monkeys,** and poisonous **snakes** are found in both environments. **An African** living in rural areas knows a greater variety of animals than **an American** living in the rural U.S. does.

Adverbs and adverbial phrases can be added to indicate the certainty of the writer or to make the statements more modest.

This city **possibly** needs to consider expansion of its public transportation **if such changes can be made without additional taxes.**

☞ **Practice 1**

Correct the verbs in the following paragraph.

Dictionaries

[1]Dictionaries are valuable tools. [2]However, as with all tools, they are valuable only when someone use them correctly. [3]A student need to understand the types of information that a dictionary provide. [4]Most dictionaries supplies more than definitions and spelling. [5]They also are giving information about pronunciation and grammar. [6]Other information includes synonyms, parts of irregular verbs, and plural forms of irregular nouns.

General Truth and Generalizations

☛ **Practice 2**

Underline the uses of *will* in the following essay. In which of these sentences can a simple present tense verb be substituted because the meaning refers to general truth rather than to future time?

Good Teachers

¹I like being a student and enjoy learning from a good teacher. ²Good teachers, to me, like to teach. ³For them, teaching is not only a job but something that they enjoy doing. ⁴They also care about their students.

⁵Some people will become teachers because they cannot find anything better to do, but others will become teachers because they enjoy teaching. ⁶Those in the second group will take their jobs more seriously. ⁷They will not lecture on the same materials over and over again but will look for new ideas, new technology, and new methods to teach better. ⁸They will begin classes on time, and they will try to make every class interesting. ⁹I recommend choosing classes with good teachers because students will learn more from teachers who like to teach than from teachers who do not enjoy teaching.

¹⁰Good teachers also care about their students. ¹¹They will care whether their students understand the lectures and whether their students need more help. ¹²Teachers in this group will make themselves available outside of class for students who need additional help. ¹³They will also take their time to listen to students' problems and give them advice.

¹⁴Good teachers will motivate and challenge their students. ¹⁵They provide interesting assignments. ¹⁶When I enter graduate school next year, these are the standards that I will use to choose courses and teachers.

Other Units Related to This Topic

✔ **2.** Subject-Verb Agreement

✔ **6.** Generic Meaning for Nouns and Articles

✔**23.** Subordinating Conjunctions and Types of Subordination

✔**33.** Present Time Writing: Present Progressive and Stative Verbs

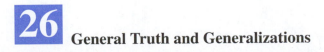

26 **General Truth and Generalizations** **181**

Irregular Verbs

Irregular verbs are verbs that do not follow the regular pattern of forming the past and the past participle with *+ed.* Irregular verbs are words like *write* (*wrote, written*) or *buy* (*bought, bought*) or *let* (*let, let*). Regular and irregular verbs make the *+ing* form in the same ways; the *+ing* form is given on this chart to make it complete.

The Basic Forms of Irregular Verbs in Alphabetical Order

Base Form	Simple Past	Past Participle	*+ing* Form
arise	*arose*	*arisen*	*arising*
awake	*awoke*	*awoke/awakened*	*awaking*
be	*was/were*	*been*	*being*
bear	*bore*	*born*	*bearing*
beat	*beat*	*beaten*	*beating*
become	*became*	*become*	*becoming*
begin	*began*	*begun*	*beginning*
bend	*bent*	*bent*	*bending*
bet	*bet*	*bet*	*betting*
bid	*bid*	*bid*	*bidding*
bind	*bound*	*bound*	*binding*
bite	*bit*	*bitten*	*biting*
bleed	*bled*	*bled*	*bleeding*
blow	*blew*	*blown*	*blowing*

Base Form	Simple Past	Past Participle	+*ing* Form
break	*broke*	*broken*	*breaking*
breed	*bred*	*bred*	*breeding*
bring	*brought*	*brought*	*bringing*
broadcast	*broadcast*	*broadcast*	*broadcasting*
build	*built*	*built*	*building*
burn	*burned/burnt*	*burned/burnt*	*burning*
burst	*burst*	*burst*	*bursting*
buy	*bought*	*bought*	*buying*
cast	*cast*	*cast*	*casting*
catch	*caught*	*caught*	*catching*
choose	*chose*	*chosen*	*choosing*
cling	*clung*	*clung*	*clinging*
come	*came*	*come*	*coming*
cost	*cost*	*cost*	*costing*
creep	*crept*	*crept*	*creeping*
cut	*cut*	*cut*	*cutting*
deal	*dealt*	*dealt*	*dealing*
dig	*dug*	*dug*	*digging*
dive	*dived/dove*	*dived*	*diving*
do	*did*	*done*	*doing*
draw	*drew*	*drawn*	*drawing*
dream	*dreamed/dreamt*	*dreamed/dreamt*	*dreaming*
drink	*drank*	*drunk*	*drinking*
drive	*drove*	*driven*	*driving*
eat	*ate*	*eaten*	*eating*
fall	*fell*	*fallen*	*falling*
feed	*fed*	*fed*	*feeding*
feel	*felt*	*felt*	*feeling*
fight	*fought*	*fought*	*fighting*
find	*found*	*found*	*finding*
fit	*fit*	*fit*	*fitting*
flee	*fled*	*fled*	*fleeing*
fling	*flung*	*flung*	*flinging*
fly	*flew*	*flown*	*flying*
forbid	*forbade*	*forbidden*	*forbidding*
forecast	*forecast*	*forecast*	*forecasting*

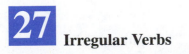

Base Form	Simple Past	Past Participle	+*ing* Form
forget	*forgot*	*forgotten*	*forgetting*
forgive	*forgave*	*forgiven*	*forgiving*
forsake	*forsook*	*forsaken*	*forsaking*
freeze	*froze*	*frozen*	*freezing*
get	*got*	*gotten*	*getting*
give	*gave*	*given*	*giving*
go	*went*	*gone*	*going*
grind	*ground*	*ground*	*grinding*
grow	*grew*	*grown*	*growing*
hang	*hung*	*hung*	*hanging*
have	*had*	*had*	*having*
hear	*heard*	*heard*	*hearing*
hide	*hid*	*hidden*	*hiding*
hit	*hit*	*hit*	*hitting*
hold	*held*	*held*	*holding*
hurt	*hurt*	*hurt*	*hurting*
keep	*kept*	*kept*	*keeping*
kneel	*knelt*	*knelt*	*kneeling*
knit	*knit*	*knit*	*knitting*
know	*knew*	*known*	*knowing*
lay	*laid*	*lain*	*laying*
lead	*led*	*led*	*leading*
leap	*leaped/leapt*	*leaped/leapt*	*leaping*
leave	*left*	*left*	*leaving*
lend	*lent*	*lent*	*lending*
let	*let*	*let*	*letting*
lie	*lay*	*laid*	*lying*
light	*lit*	*lit*	*lighting*
lose	*lost*	*lost*	*losing*
make	*made*	*made*	*making*
mean	*meant*	*meant*	*meaning*
meet	*met*	*met*	*meeting*
mislay	*mislaid*	*mislaid*	*mislaying*
mistake	*mistook*	*mistaken*	*mistaking*
mow	*mowed*	*mowed*	*mowing*

 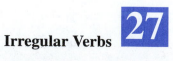

Base Form	Simple Past	Past Participle	+*ing* Form
overcome	*overcame*	*overcome*	*overcoming*
pay	*paid*	*paid*	*paying*
prove	*proved*	*proven*	*proving*
put	*put*	*put*	*putting*
quit	*quit*	*quit*	*quitting*
read	*read*	*read*	*reading*
rid	*rid*	*rid*	*ridding*
ride	*rode*	*ridden*	*riding*
ring	*rang*	*rung*	*ringing*
rise	*rose*	*risen*	*rising*
run	*ran*	*run*	*running*
say	*said*	*said*	*saying*
see	*saw*	*seen*	*seeing*
seek	*sought*	*sought*	*seeking*
sell	*sold*	*sold*	*selling*
send	*sent*	*sent*	*sending*
set	*set*	*set*	*setting*
sew	*sewed*	*sewed/sewn*	*sewing*
shake	*shook*	*shaken*	*shaking*
shave	*shaved*	*shaved/shaven*	*shaving*
shear	*shore*	*shorn*	*shearing*
shed	*shed*	*shed*	*shedding*
shine	*shone/shined*	*shone*	*shining*
shoot	*shot*	*shot*	*shooting*
show	*showed*	*shown*	*showing*
shrink	*shrank*	*shrunk*	*shrinking*
shut	*shut*	*shut*	*shutting*
sing	*sang*	*sung*	*singing*
sink	*sank*	*sunk*	*sinking*
sit	*sat*	*sat*	*sitting*
sleep	*slept*	*slept*	*sleeping*
slide	*slid*	*slid*	*sliding*
slit	*slit*	*slit*	*slitting*
sow	*sowed*	*sown*	*sowing*
speak	*spoke*	*spoken*	*speaking*

Base Form	Simple Past	Past Participle	+ing Form
speed	sped	sped	speeding
spend	spent	spent	spending
spin	spun	spun	spinning
spit	spit	spit	spitting
split	split	split	splitting
spread	spread	spread	spreading
spring	sprung	sprang	springing
stand	stood	stood	standing
steal	stolen	stole	stealing
stick	stuck	stuck	sticking
sting	stung	stung	stinging
stink	stunk	stank	stinking
strike	struck	struck	striking
string	strung	strung	stringing
swear	swore	sworn	swearing
sweep	swept	swept	sweeping
swell	swelled	swelled/swollen	swelling
swim	swam	swum	swimming
swing	swung	swung	swinging
take	took	taken	taking
teach	taught	taught	teaching
tear	tore	torn	tearing
tell	told	told	telling
think	thought	thought	thinking
throw	threw	thrown	throwing
thrust	thrust	thrust	thrusting
understand	understood	understood	understanding
wake	woke	woken	waking
wear	wore	worn	wearing
weave	wove	woven	weaving
weep	wept	wept	weeping
win	won	won	winning
withdraw	withdrew	withdrawn	withdrawing
wring	wrung	wrung	wringing
write	wrote	written	writing

Irregular Verbs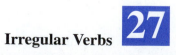

☛ Practice

You would probably benefit from looking over the entire list of irregular verbs to find out for yourself which ones are still problems for you. Try putting a sheet of paper over the list to cover all but the first form; write the other three forms on the paper, and then check to see which ones you misspelled or whose meanings you do not know.

Other Units Related to This Topic

27 **Irregular Verbs**

Modal Auxiliary Verbs

Basic Modal Auxiliary Verbs

can	*could*
may	*might*
must	
shall	*should*
will	*would*

Traditional Definitions for the Modal Auxiliary Verbs

You will often find the following words used to define the modal auxiliary verbs. Some students like to memorize these definitions, so they are presented here with sample sentences for convenient review.

Verb	Traditional Definition	Example
can	ability	I **can type**.
	request	**Can** I **borrow** a pen?
	permission	You **can use** your dictionaries on the test.
	possibility	You **can take** calculus in the spring if you want to.
could	present time request	**Could** you **take** a message?
	present time possibility	That answer **could be** right.
	past time ability (no longer true)	I **could type** faster when I was in typing class.
	past time possibility	The test **could have been** even harder.
		I **could have gone** to the party last Saturday, but I decided to go to a movie instead.
may	present time request	**May** I **leave** early?
	present time permission	You **may leave** early.
	present time probability	Suwan was tired yesterday; he **may be** tired right now.
	future time probability	He **may come** to the meeting tonight, but he is not sure that he can leave work early.
	past time probability	Suwan **may have worked** the night shift last night. He often does.

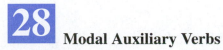

Verb	Traditional Definition	Example
might	present time (slight probability)	Suwan **might be** sick, but he **might** just **be** tired.
	future time (slight probability)	We **might get** our test papers back in class tomorrow.
	past time probability	Suwan **might have gone** to the library last night. He planned to, but I did not see him there.
shall	polite question	**Shall** we **leave** now?
	future time (formal style)	In this chapter, **we shall discuss** management theory.
should	advice (general truth)	You **should eat** a good breakfast every morning.
	future time expectation	It is 7:45 right now. The bus **should be** here at 8:05.
	obligation (general truth)	We **should respect** the opinions of other people.
	past time advice	You **should have gotten** more sleep before the exam. You were too tired to think clearly.
must	necessity (general truth)	Students **must have** health insurance.
	future time necessity	You **must arrive** early tomorrow in order to go to the library before class.

Modal Auxiliary Verbs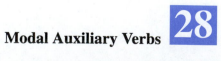

Verb	Traditional Definition	Example
	logical deduction (certainty)	He **must be** tired. He seems to have no energy, and he keeps yawning.
	past time logical deduction (certainty)	Suwan made a perfect score on the calculus test. He **must have studied** very hard.
will	general truth	Oil **will float** on water.
	future time intention	I **will study** for the test after I get home from the meeting.
	future time promise	I **will meet** you after class to study for the test.
	future time certainty	Our final examination **will be** on December 12.
would	conditional (general truth)	If I were you, I **would use** my dictionary more often.
	polite request	**Would** you **please** loan me a pen?
	preference (general truth)	I **would rather study** chemistry than history.
	past time habit	Last year we **would study** together every weekend. This year, I work in the library on Saturday and Sunday.
	past time preference	I **would rather have studied** chemistry than history, but the history course was required for graduation.

Meanings of the Semi-Modals

Semi-Modal is the name for a small group of verbs that are like the modal auxiliaries in meaning but unlike them in grammar. Compare the examples of semi-modals to the examples given earlier in this unit for the modals with the same meaning.

Basic Modal	Semi-Modal Synonym	Traditional Definition	Example
can	*be able to*	ability	Juan **is able to speak** both Spanish and Catalan.
		possibility	Because we live in the mountains, we **can go** skiing every winter.
should	*ought to*	duty or obligation	I **ought to work** on my project this afternoon, but I do not really want to.
should	*had better*	strong advice	You **had better talk** with your advisor about your schedule before you choose your classes for next quarter.
must	*have to*	necessity or requirement	All students **have to buy** medical insurance.

Modal Auxiliary Verbs 28

Grammar of *Be Able To*

Be able to is like the modal *can* in its meaning. However, it has two major differences in grammar.
1. *Be able to* requires subject-verb agreement.
2. It also uses the word *to*.

Students **are able to** check out books from the library for a three-week period.

At this university, a student **is able to use** the computer lab for free just by showing her/his picture identification card.

Be able to is useful as a synonym for *can* because the semi-modal can be combined with one of the basic modals to get both meanings in one verb phrase.

Next quarter we **will be able to use** the library later in the evenings because the closing time will be extended to 12 midnight.

Grammar of *Ought To* and *Had Better*

Ought to and *had better* are like *should* in meaning. *Ought to* is different in grammar because it requires the word *to*. *Ought to* is not often used in formal contexts and is used more in speaking than in writing.

Dr. Jones said, "You **ought to study** harder for the final examination than you did for the mid-term."

Had better always uses the past tense form *had* and never uses *to*. In spoken English *had* is often contracted.

Students **had better not park** in the spaces reserved for faculty members. The fine is a lot of money.

You**'d better pay** that library fine right away, or you won't be able to register for classes.

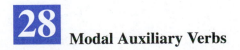

28 **Modal Auxiliary Verbs**

Grammar of *Have To*

For general truth and future time meanings, *must* and *have to* both refer to necessities and requirements. *Have to* is different grammatically from *must* in two important ways: (1) subject-verb agreement rules must be followed, and (2) *to* is required.

Accounting students **have to take** Calculus 302.

Each student **has to pass** English 101 before taking any courses in her/his major field.

Have to also has a past tense form. *Had to* refers to past time necessities. In contrast, *must have* + past participle has a completely different meaning and refers to guesses about past time events.

It was necessary to take the test two times, and then I could drive.

I **had to take** the driver's license test two times before I passed it.

The writer does not know what happened to Roseanne and is making a guess rather than making a statement of fact.

Roseanne did not come to the final examination yesterday afternoon. She **must have been** very sick to miss such an important test.

Grammar of *Would Rather*

Would rather is used to state preferences in a polite manner. Like *would,* this semi-modal is followed by an infinitive without *to.* Notice that the verb does not have to be repeated if the same verb is used twice. To answer a question with this semi-modal, you need only to give the short form for your choice. (The answer does not have to repeat the exact words of the question.)

I **would rather take** physics than **take** history.

I **would rather take** physics than history.

Would you rather have dinner now or **go** to the library first? I **would rather eat** first.

Problems with Modal Auxiliaries

Problem 1

Using *to* with modals

Problem	Solution	Revision
*Her children will always know that they **can to go** to her for advice or help.	The basic modals combine with a verb without using *to*. Remove *to* for the revision.	Her children will always know that they **can go** to her for advice or help.

Problem 2

Adding +*s* to the verb in modal + verb combination

Problem	Solution	Revision
*A student **can uses** computers for many purposes.	The basic modals do not require subject-verb agreement. The writer has two choices for revision: (1) remove +*s,* and make a statement about possibilities for students. (2) Remove the modal, and make a general truth statement about modern students.	A student **can use** computers for many purposes. A student **uses** computers for many purposes.

Problem 3

Using two modals together in the same verb phrase

Problem	Solution	Revision
*He **might can take** tennis next summer.	Some dialects of English can combine two modals in one verb phrase for spoken uses. This combination is not appropriate for formal written English. Substitute *be able to* for *can.*	He **might be able to take** tennis next summer.

28 **Modal Auxiliary Verbs**

Problem 4

Adding +ed to the verb in a modal + verb combination

Problem	Solution	Revision
*I do not like to spend so much money on textbooks. I **can used** the money for something else.	The modal + verb combination requires the simple, base form of the verb. Remove +d to return to the base form *use*.	I do not like to spend so much money on textbooks. I **can use** the money for something else.
*If I created these new categories, I **could separated** the data into three subdivisions.	The writer wants to make a hypothetical statement. Therefore, a past tense form of the verb is required in the *if*-clause. The main verb combines *could* with a base form of the verb. Remove +d to have the base verb *separate*.	If I created these new categories, I **could separate** the data into three subdivisions.

Problem 5

Not using a past participle in a modal + passive combination

Problem	Solution	Revision
*Water that you use to bathe your child **can be reuse** to water your garden.	The active form is *you can reuse water.* The passive form is *water can be reused.* Add +d to make the past participle.	Water that you use to bathe your child **can be reused** to water your garden.
*At some supermarkets, computers **can be find** even on the carts.	The active form is *you can find computers.* The passive form is *computers can be found.* Use the correct past participle.	At some supermarkets, computers **can be found** even on the carts.

Problem 6

Not using the correct words when combining modal + *be* + present participle

Problem	Solution	Revision
*I do not know what I want to major in. I hope I make a decision soon. I **might still deciding** next year.	The writer wants to combine *might* with the progressive for a future time meaning. However, *be* was left out. Revise the sentence by adding *be*.	I do not know what I want to major in. I hope I make a decision soon. I **might still be deciding** next year.
*If I had had the freedom to choose my own courses, I **would finishing** my college career much earlier.	The writer is trying to make a hypothetical statement about future time. The revision can either (1) add *be* or (2) remove +*ing*. The two versions mean nearly the same thing.	If I had had the freedom to choose my own courses, I **would be finishing** my college career much earlier. If I had had the freedom to choose my own courses, I **would finish** my college career much earlier.

☞ **Practice 1**

For each sentence, circle the letter of the option that correctly completes each sentence.

1. I _____ better complete at least seventy-five hours before I transfer to another university.

   (a) had   (b) should   (c) would

2. I have completed sixty college credits, so next year, I will _____ transfer to Iowa State University.

   (a) can   (b) be supposed to   (c) be able to

3. I _____ rather study at a small college than at a large university.

   (a) can   (b) should   (c) would

4. I did not do well on the mid-term test. I _____ studied more.

    (a) ought to   (b) should have   (c) must

5. I could not speak English last year, but I _____ now.

    (a) can   (b) can be able to   (c) can do

6. My roommate's English is improving, and next year, my roommate will _____ take regular college classes.

    (a) can   (b) be able to   (c) had to

7. When I lived in my country, I _____ live in my parents' home, but in the United States I live with a roommate in an apartment.

    (a) must not   (b) might   (c) could

8. Before I transfer to Iowa State University, I _____ send the university a copy of my transcript.

    (a) must to   (b) need   (c) must

9. Right now I _____ work on getting my GPA (grade point average) as high as possible.

    (a) ought   (b) should   (c) had to

10. Next quarter I _____ only two courses.

    (a) might take   (b) might will take   (c) might have taken

☞ Practice 2

Underline the verb phrases in each of the following sentences. Make any corrections that are necessary.

1. I cannot imagine that things like this would happens.

2. When I got tired of studying, I would thinking about my father's advice, and I would studying again.

3. I wish that I could saw my parents frequently.

4. Using this system, I could easily evaluated the performance of my teachers.

5. I was born with musical talent. As a child, I could played anything that I heard my teacher play.

6. In my home country if students wear clothes other than jeans, they must came from a rich family.

7. If students communicated well using the skills that they learned in school, they would felt that they were well educated.

8. During the storm, we lost all electricity in my neighborhood. All I could saw was darkness.

9. If I knew that my life would soon end, I would traveled around the world.

10. If I won the lottery, there are three important ways in which my life would to change.

11. At my supermarket, they put a small computer on each cart to show customers where an item can be fined.

12. If its leader does not know how to run an organization, it might be destroy.

13. I think that every teacher should be prepare for class and should be able answer the students' questions about the content for that class.

14. All elementary school teachers should has a bachelor's degree.

15. Although some of the courses that I took were not required for my major, I took them to increase my knowledge of biology. As a result, I will well prepared for my career.

Other Units Related to This Topic

Modal Auxiliaries for Advice, Recommendations, and Rules

Modal Auxiliaries Used for Giving Advice, Making Recommendations, and Stating Rules

When used to give advice or make recommendations, the modal auxiliaries have a systematic relationship based on meaning. You select a modal based on the strength of your advice.

	Modal	Meaning	Example
weaker	*can,* *could,* *may,* or *might*	These are your choices, or this action is possible. Notice that the titles of the movies are underlined; see Unit 57 for more information.	You and your roommate are talking about the two movies that you both want to see: We can go to <u>Batman Returns</u> this weekend and then see <u>Howards End</u> next week. In giving the directions for a test, your instructor gives you a choice: You may write on either topic A or topic B.

Modal	Meaning	Example

stronger
 	
should
or
ought to
	This is very good advice, or this is your responsibility.	To explain your ideas on improvements needed by your university, you write:
		`The university should provide more sections of calculus in the evening.`
		
		A good friend is concerned about your grades and says to you:
		`You ought to study more and watch TV less.`

stronger
 	
must
or
have to
	This action is required. This is the law. There are no good choices. You will have serious problems if you ignore this advice.	The regulations for the university state:
		`All international students have to buy medical insurance.`
		
		On the parking ticket are these words:
		`This fine must be paid no later than January 15.`

stronger *will*	There is no choice. This advice is so strong that the form is almost never used. Few people have the power to make such strong statements to other people.	The young man's father says to him: `As long as you live in my house, you will be home before 11:00 p.m.`

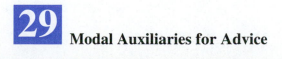

☞ Practice 1

Read the following paragraph, and underline each modal. Then, correct five of the modals you underlined.

Advice for a Friend

¹If a friend of mine wants to come to the United States, I will advised her to study English, to learn how to drive a car, and to come to Kansas City. ²She will need to learn to speak English as quickly as possible because she must be able to speak English in order to find a place to live, to take college courses, and to get a driver's license. ³And, of course, if she goes shopping, she should knows how to ask the price of things. ⁴The United states is a big place, and it will be very difficult for her to get around if she cannot drive. ⁵If she has a driver's license before she comes, she might not had to take a driving test. ⁶I will also advised her to come to Kansas City because there are many Japanese students here and because there are good colleges here. ⁷She might want to choose a college that has special English classes. ⁸If my friend decides to come to the United States, she should to follow my advice.

☞ Practice 2

Read the following paragraph, and underline each modal. Then, make the needed corrections.

Advice for a Longer Life

¹Would you like to live a longer life? ²To live longer, doctors say that you must to keep your body healthy, and here are some hints that may help you. ³First, you had to eat healthy foods that will provides necessary proteins, vitamins, and carbohydrates. ⁴You had better not to eat food that contains a great deal of fat and cholesterol because they are the main substances that can to cause heart attacks. ⁵A proper diet can keep your body healthy. ⁶The second important requirement is regular exercise. ⁷You should to exercise every day. ⁸You might jog or lift weights to keep your body healthy and active. ⁹The third and most important point is not to take illegal drugs. ¹⁰Drugs might ruin your life and the lives of your family. ¹¹You should not smokes, and you should not to take heroin, morphine, or cocaine. ¹²By keeping your body healthy now while you are young, you could have lived longer and ought enjoy life more.

Other Units Related to This Topic

Modal Auxiliaries for Advice

30

Modal Auxiliaries for Logical Probability and for Making Guesses

Modal Auxiliaries for Making Guesses

Used when giving explanations for unclear situations, events, or actions, the modal auxiliaries have a systematic relationship based on meaning. You select a modal based on the strength of your belief in your explanation.

	Modal	Meaning	Example
weaker	*could,* *may,* or *might*	The speaker gives a reasonable explanation but is not certain about who is at the door.	You are in the living room of your apartment talking with your roommate. You hear a knock on the front door. You say to your roommate: "That **might** be my sister. She planned to come here after class if possible. But I don't really expect her because she needed to go grocery shopping."

	Modal	Meaning	Example
stronger	*should* or *ought to*	The speaker is expecting Jack and feels that this statement is a good explanation for the knock at the door. However, the speaker is not completely certain about who is at the door.	You are in the living room of your apartment talking with your roommate. You are expecting a friend to arrive very soon to work on a research project together. You hear a knock at the door and say to your roommate: "That **should** be Jack. He was supposed to be here at 2:00."
stronger	*must* or *have to*	This sentence shows a very strong explanation with little room for doubt.	You are in the living room of your apartment talking with your roommate. You ordered a pizza about thirty minutes ago. You hear a knock on the front door. You say to your roommate: "That **must** be the pizza. They usually take about thirty minutes."
stronger	*will*	The speaker has almost no doubt about who is at the door. This is a statement of certainty.	You are in the living room of your apartment talking with your roommate. You hear familiar footsteps on the stairs and a special rhythm is knocked on the door. You know from past experience that the person outside is your brother. You are still guessing because you have not looked to see who is really outside the door. Your say to your roommate: "**That'll** be Mohammed. He always knocks on the door like that."
stronger	*be* or some verb	The speaker is sure about the explanation. There is no doubt at all.	You are in the living room of your apartment talking with your roommate. You hear a knock on the door. You get up and look through the peephole to see who is there. You say to your roommate: "**It's** Mary from downstairs. I wonder what she wants."

Modal Auxiliaries for Logical Probability

☞ **Practice**

Write an explanation for each of these situations using an appropriate modal.

1. You are asleep. It is late at night. The telephone rings. What do you think?

2. You are at home. You are eating dinner. You hear a knock at the front door. What do you think?

3. The radio news says that there is a 90 percent chance of rain for the weekend. You are supposed to have a picnic with friends from school. What are your choices?

4. The newspaper has a story about the president of a local bank. He has been arrested for stealing $100,000 from the bank. What do you think?

5. You have to pay your tuition tomorrow. The check for your tuition has not arrived yet. What are your choices?

6. You are sitting in class. You remember that you left your homework paper on your desk at home. What are your choices?

7. It is the break between terms. Your school sends grades to students in the mail. You get an envelope in your mail with the school's return address in the upper left-hand corner. It is official stationery. What do you think?

8. You receive your statement for your checking account. You thought that you had $135 left. The statement shows $56.75. What do you think? What do you do?

9. You get your mid-term test paper back. You expected to make a "B." The grade is "C." What do you think? What do you do?

10. You are in the school cafeteria eating lunch with some friends. A man wearing a short white jacket and a stethoscope enters the room. Who is the man?

Other Units Related to This Topic

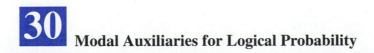

30 **Modal Auxiliaries for Logical Probability**   **205**

Modal Auxiliaries and Past Time Writing

Modals and Past Time

Could + verb and *would* + verb can be used to refer to past time abilities or habits that are no longer true in the present.

Last quarter, I **could ride** to class with my sister, but she graduated. Now I must take the bus.

When my grandmother was alive, she **would prepare** wonderful traditional food for our dinner.

Any of the modal auxiliaries can combine with *have* + past participle for past time meanings.

He **could have taken** calculus this quarter but decided to wait until next year.

They **may have gone** to the library, but I do not know where they are.

I **should have gone** to the supermarket yesterday, but I did not have time. Now we are out of coffee.

Could + verb means "past time ability that has been lost." *Could* + *have* + past participle means "past time ability or possibility that was not done." Although they both refer to past time, the two examples are very different in meaning: *could play* means that "I played tennis well in the past but I cannot play so well now." *Could have gone* means that I "did not go, but I had the possibility of going."	I **could play** tennis well when I was a teenager, but I have not played in many years. I **could have gone** to the library, but I decided to stay home to study here.
Would + verb refers to a past time habit. *Would* + *have* + past participle refers to a conditional possibility that did not happen. My father cut the wood when he was a child—it happened then but does not happen now. Juan did not take the test although he was prepared to take it.	When my father was a child, he **would chop** wood for his mother to use in her stove. That was one of his jobs to help his family. Juan **would have taken** the test this morning, but he was sick.

Negation and Past Time Modals

When *not* is added, these phrases reverse their meaning. *I could have gone* means "I did not go." *I could not have come* means that "I did come."	I **could have gone** to the party, but I did not have enough time. I **could not have come** to this university to study without a scholarship.
When combined with *have* + past participle, *must* is limited to its "logical probability" meaning. The sentence is a strong guess about the past.	Maria made a perfect score on the calculus final examination. She **must have studied** very hard. I did not see Jose at the reception for new students. He **must not have attended**.

Modal Auxiliaries and Past Time Writing 207

In these verb combinations, *should + have* + past participle refers to a past time obligation that was neglected. It can refer to advice that was not taken. The negative version is used to communicate about things that were done that were mistakes.

I **should have eaten** breakfast before I came to school. I am really hungry now.

I **should not have eaten** that third piece of cake. I feel sick.

Would + have + past participle refers to past time conditions and possibilities that were not done.

I studied for the test. I knew the material thoroughly. I **would have taken** the test, and I **would have made** a very good grade. However, I got sick that morning and had to stay at home.

Would + have + past participle refers to a past time certainty, while *should + have* + past participle refers to past time advice or obligations or responsibilities.

I am sorry that I missed the reception for new students. I **would have gone**; I had planned to go, but I had to work.

I **should have written** a letter to my sister this morning. It is my responsibility to write her every week. However, I just did not have time because I had to study for the test. I will write her tonight.

Modal Auxiliaries and Past Time Writing

Correct the verbs in the following sentences, as necessary; some sentences are correct.

1. The only thing that I would have change about my childhood would be my lack of exercise.

2. I should taken time out to become more involved in sports during my teenage years.

3. My friends may has been more involved in sports than I was.

4. When I was a child, I would spend my time watching television and eating junk food.

5. When I was seven, my parents decided that I should have left home to go to a private school in Seoul.

6. I remember clearly one night in 1992 when all of a sudden the television turned off, and all I could saw was darkness.

7. I should not have spend my tuition money on my trip to California.

8. I should have checked my grades on Friday, so I would not have had to wait until Monday.

9. If I had been asked to evaluate my teachers last semester, I would have use two standards: their interest in teaching and their knowledge of their subjects.

10. Some historians say that World War II could been avoid had important decisions and agreements been made on time.

Other Units Related to This Topic

Past Time Writing: Past Tense, Past Perfect, and Past Progressive

Verb Choices for Past Time Writing

Generally, past time meaning is best expressed using the *simple past tense* form of a verb.

`Fleming `**`discovered`**` penicillin by accident.`

Past perfect has limited use. Primarily, it is used in sentences that emphasize that one event was completed in the past before another past time event. Avoid using past perfect unless it is absolutely necessary for clarity of meaning. The first two examples are both grammatically correct; they have slightly different meanings.

However, past perfect is required when *already* or *just* are included to mean "before now" in past time contexts.

`We `**`went`**` to the library before we went to the computer laboratory.`

`We `**`had gone`**` to the library before we went to the computer laboratory.`

`We `**`had already gone`**` to the library when we arrived at the computer laboratory.`

`We `**`had just completed`**` the test when time was up for class.`

Past progressive is limited to sentences that emphasize the ongoing nature of an event in the past. Often, simple past tense is used rather than the past progressive. Past progressive is a stylistic variation on the simple past tense. Avoid using many past progressive verbs in any one piece of writing. All three examples are grammatically correct; each is slightly different in its emphasis. The simple past tense gives a photograph of the event; the past progressive provides a video that shows the action. The three example sentences differ only in style and in emphasis.

Maria **studied** for the test while her roommate **cooked** dinner.

Maria **was studying** for the test while her roommate **cooked** dinner.

Maria **was studying** for the test while her roommate **was cooking** dinner.

Modal auxiliaries can be used in past time writing to indicate the writer's attitudes and level of certainty.

I feel really unhappy about the test. I **should have studied** longer. I **should not have gone** to the party.

Maria did not come to the test today. She **must have gotten** sick last night. She **should have called** the teacher to explain her problem before the test.

☞ **Practice 1**

Edit the following paragraph for past time verbs.

A Vacation in Hawaii

¹Last summer, my sister and I went to Hawaii to relax. ²We chose Hawaii because we do not have any friends or relatives there, so we can enjoy our vacation without any interruptions. ³In Hawaii, the beaches that we visit seem cleaner than the beaches in Florida, and a lot of palm trees surround the beaches. ⁴At one beach, we saw the Hawaiians made a circle, and they danced one by one within the circle. ⁵We enjoyed watching the dances and at the same time had a fresh coconut drink. ⁶Every night that we stayed in Hawaii, there are shows near the beaches, and the shows that we saw are marvelous. ⁷However, we enjoyed the ocean the most. ⁸We plan to go to Hawaii again next summer because it is a good place to visit, and everything was cheaper than at home.

32 **Past Time Writing**

☞ **Practice 2**

Edit the following paragraph for past time verbs.

My Job Last Summer

¹Last summer I worked in a laundry which was only three blocks from my apartment. ²While I work there, I enjoy my work very much. ³My boss is friendly, helpful, and kind to me. ⁴The first day that I worked there, he taught me many things. ⁵For example, he taught me how to use a washing machine and a dryer and how to fold and iron clothes. ⁶Whenever I made a mistake, he never become angry; instead, he told me what I should have done so that I will not make the same mistake again. ⁷Most of the time, he had a hard time understanding my English; however, this did not change the way he treat me. ⁸He correct my English mistakes and always encourage me to read the newspaper more and to watch the nightly news on television. ⁹After one month of work, school started, so I quitted my job and prepared to start my new quarter of college. ¹⁰I enjoy myself very much while I work there.

☞ **Practice 3**

Edit the following paragraph for past time verbs.

Adjusting to My Life in the United States

¹I came to the United States to get an education, but before I came here, I did not know very much about American colleges and universities. ²There are several adjustments that I have to make, but now I feel comfortable in school here. ³I remember that I get lost on the way to the campus; however, I find it after two hours of driving around the area. ⁴When I look for the Administration Building, I could not find it because it was moved temporarily to another building while the offices are being renovated. ⁵Finally, I found the right office, applied to the college, and was accepted. ⁶On the first day of school, I woke up early, took a shower, drank some coffee, and drove to college. ⁷It is seven o'clock in the morning, and only the security people were in the Student Center. ⁸I thought that colleges in the United States, like in my country, started early and that students dressed up for classes. ⁹For example, we were not permitted to wear shorts or short-sleeved shirts to school in my country. ¹⁰When I first see my American classmates wearing shorts, I am embarrassed. ¹¹Moreover in my country, we are not allowed to drink, eat, or chew gum in classes. ¹²When I saw my classmates drinking soda or chewing gum, it is very surprising to me. ¹³The most embarrassing situation was when my teacher call my name and I stand up as I used to do in my country; everyone stare at me.

Correct thirteen verbs in the following paragraph.

Two Problems

¹I have faced two problems since I came to the United States. ²When I first arrived, people talked so fast that it is hard for me to understand what they have said. ³In addition, when I talked to them, they could not understand me. ⁴I get angry with myself because I could not talk to anyone. ⁵A year ago, I ask my teacher about my problem, and she tell me that my English pronunciation was hard to understand. ⁶She teached me how to pronounce some hard sounds and some different vocabulary words. ⁷As a result, now I was able to talk with American students. ⁸Two years ago I am not able to understand spoken English because Americans, besides speaking very fast, using many difficult words. ⁹When someone begin to talk to me, I always have to ask that person to speak slower and to repeat everything. ¹⁰However, now I could understand almost everything because I watch television every day and because I spend many hours last year in special English classes for foreign students. ¹¹Even though I speak and understand English better now, I still have problems.

Other Units Related to This Topic

✔**27.** Irregular Verbs

✔**28.** Modal Auxiliary Verbs

✔**31.** Modal Auxiliaries and Past Time Writing

✔**35.** Sequence of Tense and Reported Speech

✔**36.** Subjunctive Verbs

32 **Past Time Writing**

33

Present Time Writing: Present Progressive and Stative Verbs

Present Time Verb Choices

Present progressive is used with action verbs for present time meaning. *Action verbs* are any verbs that refer to activities.

My brother **is studying** English grammar and writing this quarter. He **is** also **taking** a course in calculus.

You **are reading** this example right now.

Simple present tense is used with stative verbs for present time meaning. *Stative verbs* are any verbs that refer to states of being rather than to actions.

Ben **knows** Spanish and Chinese.

This book **weighs** less than two pounds.

Stative Verbs

Stative is a kind of meaning that a verb can have. Many verbs can be either "stative" or "active," depending on the intended meaning. Some verbs are usually used for stative meaning. These are listed below. However, even these verbs can change to be used for actions.

state of being
This coffee **tastes** good.

action
I **am tasting** this coffee.

state of being
You **appear** tired and unhappy.

action
```
Jane Alexander is appearing
in a new play at the campus
theater.
```

Be is often used for stative meaning. It can refer to both permanent and temporary states of being.

```
She is in the laboratory.

My hometown is in Nova
Scotia.
```

Stative Verb Categories

Senses	Mental States	Emotions	Ownership Possession Relationship	Measuring
appear	believe	appreciate	belong	cost
feel	doubt	desire	contain	equal
hear	imagine	dislike	have	measure
look (to mean "appear")	know	hate	own	weigh
see	mean	like		
smell	recognize	love		
taste	remember	need		
	suppose	prefer		
	think	seem		
	understand	want		
	wonder			

☛ **Practice 1**

Place a check by each verb below that is usually used for stative meaning.

1. _____ annoy

2. _____ dislike

3. _____ have

4. _____ enjoy

5. _____ cost

6. _____ identify

7. _____ like

8. _____ recognize

9. _____ appear

10. _____ become

11. _____ watch

12. _____ think

33 Present Time Writing

☛ Practice 2

Choose the correct form of each verb in the following sentences: present progressive or simple present tense. In some sentences, both forms are possible.

1. The calculator on the desk is belonging/belongs to my teacher.

2. Everyone in my class is knowing/knows how to use WordPerfect.

3. I am enjoying/enjoy my math class this quarter.

4. My roommate is taking/takes calculus next quarter.

5. I am thinking/think that I will not take calculus until next year.

☛ Practice 3

Correct any problems with the verbs in the following paragraph.

What Is It?

[1]The object that I am wanting to describe is black and thin, and it is about five inches in length. [2]I am using this object every day. [3]The object is having many small buttons on it; the buttons have some math numbers and symbols on them. [4]A small screen displays numbers when I touch the different buttons. [5]The left side of the object has an on-and-off switch which I am using frequently. [6]This object has many parts to describe, and I want to discuss a few of them. [7]In the center of the first line are these words: *sin, cos,* and *tan.* [8]Under these three buttons, the important *log* button is appearing. [9]Finally, the ten number keys, which I use every day, and the four function keys of division, multiplication, subtraction, and addition are completing the front of this object. [10]On the back, there is a small access door for two batteries. [11]I am sure that you recognizing this object as a calculator.

Other Units Related to This Topic

✔ **2.** Subject-Verb Agreement

✔**26.** General Truth and Generalizations: Present Tense

Present Perfect Verb Form

Basic Meaning of Present Perfect Verbs

Present perfect verbs are used to communicate indefinite past time. *Indefinite past* means "some time before now."	I **have studied** English for many years. I expect to continue to study English in two required courses: English 101 and English 102.
In contrast, simple past tense verbs refer to definite times in the past and to events that are completed.	I **took** calculus in high school, so I do not have to take it at the university.
Often, events reported with present perfect verbs can continue in the present.	I **have lived** in this city since 1985, and I plan to continue living here for at least another fifteen years. I **lived** in Toronto until 1985.
Present perfect verbs are frequently used to introduce a topic. Then, simple past tense is used when the topic turns to specific past times.	I **have visited** Paris many times. The latest visit **was** in December, 1991. It **was** extremely cold, but I just **wore** my warmest clothes and **enjoyed** myself anyway. My most expensive souvenir **was** a very bad cold.

Number of Events Possible with the Present Perfect

Continuous Actions. Present perfect verbs can refer to things that began in the past and extend to the present.

```
I have lived in this part
of the U.S. since I was
born.
```

Repeated Actions. Present perfect verbs can refer to things that happened repeatedly but not continuously in the past.

```
I have studied French for
many years.
```

A Particular Number of Times. Present perfect verbs can refer to things that happened a number of times in the indefinite past.

```
I have been to the
mountains about five times
since I moved here to
Colorado.
```

One Time. Present perfect verbs can refer to things that happened only one time in the indefinite past.

```
I have traveled to London
only one time.
```

Words and Phrases That Require the Present Perfect

Ever and *Never.* Generally, the present perfect is used with *ever* and *never.* However, in definite past time contexts, the simple past is used.

```
I have never visited
Madrid.

Has she ever been to Spain?

In his entire life, my
grandfather never left the
U.S. I do not think he ever
left the state of Wyoming
where he was born, lived,
and died.
```

Present Perfect Verb Form

For and Since. Generally, present perfect is used with time phrases made with *for* and *since*.

We have lived here **for ten years.**

I have lived here **since I got my current job at the university.**

This is the _____ time that someone has done something. Notice that the past time version of the phrase requires simple past tense and substitutes *that* for *this*.

present time version
This is the first time that I **have studied** Arabic.

present time version
This is the second time that the students **have gone** to the lab.

present time version
This is the three hundredth time that I **have paid** rent for this apartment.

past time version
That was the last time that I **talked** with him.

Yet and Already. Present perfect is generally used with *yet* and *already* because the words mean "before now." *Yet* and *already* refer to the indefinite past.

We **have** not **been** to the computer laboratory **yet.**

I **have already paid** my tuition for this quarter.

Superlatives. Present perfect is used with superlatives in statements with this pattern: ***This is the _____st thing that someone has ever done.*** These statements are seldom literal in meaning but are made to emphasize the feelings of the speaker.

That was the easiest test that I **have ever taken.**

This is the worst hamburger that I **have ever eaten.**

He is the tallest man that we **have ever seen.**

I am having the most fun that I **have ever had.**

Problems with Present Perfect Verbs

Problem 1

Using simple past tense when present perfect is required

Problem	Solution	Revision
*This chemistry course is the most difficult class that I **ever took.**	The writer is still taking the course and is still a student. The present perfect is required to mean "before now." Remove *took;* add *have taken.*	This chemistry course is the most difficult class that I **have ever taken.**

Problem 2

Not using the correct verb for subject-verb agreement

Problem	Solution	Revision
*Computer science courses **has become** very important for college students.	The writer needs to adjust either the subject or the verb to revise this sentence.	A computer science course **has become** very important for college students. Computer science courses **have become** very important for college students.

Present Perfect Verb Form

Not using the correct form of the past participle

Problem	Solution	Revision
*History **has show** that many countries gained their independence through war.	Present perfect verbs require a past participle. *Shown* is the past participle for the irregular verb *show*.	History **has shown** that many countries gained their independence through war.
*In my political science class, I **have learn** many things about politics.	Present perfect verbs require a past participle. Add +*ed* to make the past participle form *learned*.	In my political science class, I **have learned** many things about politics.

☞ **Practice 1**

Correct any problems with the verbs in the following sentences; some sentences are correct.

1. Historical events reveal that war has played an important part in the development of many countries.

2. Compromises over the years has drastically change the ways that people work together.

3. Everyone have dreams; I have always dreaming of becoming a great pianist but have never taken the time to learn to play the piano until now.

4. After I have graduated from high school in 1992, I had to decide if I would go to work or continue my education.

5. Leaving the protection of my family and country to attend college here in the United States has given me a sense of independence.

6. After I have arrived in San Francisco, I learned how to drive.

7. Since I received my driver's license, I had two traffic tickets for speeding.

8. The university that I attend, Harvard, has been existing for many years and maintaining a good academic reputation in the state as well as in the nation.

34 **Present Perfect Verb Form** **221**

☞ **Practice 2**

Put the correct verb in the correct form in the following paragraph. You may use a verb more than once: *achieve be believe earn leave return.*

Seeking Education, Fame, and Fortune

Twenty-five years ago, I _____ my home in the West Indies. My

<u>1</u>

intent at the time _____ to seek an education, _____ fame and

<u>2</u> <u>3</u>

fortune, and one day _____ home. At the age of sixteen, I _____

<u>4</u> <u>5</u>

that anything _____ possible. Now, twenty-five years later, I

<u>6</u>

_____ a college degree, but at this time fame and fortune

<u>7</u>

_____ nowhere in sight.

<u>8</u>

☞ **Practice 3**

Put the correct verb in the correct form in the following paragraph: *be build provide take teach.*

The Most Useful Courses That I Have Taken

Two of the classes that I _____ seem to me the most important

<u>1</u>

ones for accounting majors. As an accounting major, knowing about the

business field _____ very important to me, and my courses in business

<u>2</u>

administration _____ me with this knowledge. Moreover, these courses

<u>3</u>

_____ me how to communicate effectively and how to use computers

<u>4</u>

to solve business problems. I also have learned how to complete my income

tax forms. To conclude, I consider that my business administration and

accounting courses _____ my most useful university courses so far. All

<u>5</u>

these courses have provided knowledge about society and business, and they

_____ a strong base for my future accounting career.

<u>6</u>

Other Units Related to This Topic

✔ **2.** Subject-Verb Agreement

✔**32.** Past Time Writing: Past Tense, Past Perfect, and Past Progressive

Present Perfect Verb Form

35

Sequence of Tense and Reported Speech

Writing About What Other People Say

Quotation of Statements Made in the Past. Often we write about things that people said in the past. These quotations often are stated with words such as *said, stated, implied,* and *mentioned.*

Direct quotations give the exact words inside quotation marks. *Indirect quotations* rephrase the words, making necessary changes in pronouns and in verbs.

direct quotation

At the reception last night, the president of our university **said,** "I will visit our sister university in Japan next spring."

informal indirect quotation

The president of our university **said** yesterday that he **will visit** our sister university in Japan next spring.

formal indirect quotation

The president of our university **said** yesterday that he **would visit** our sister university in Japan next spring.

General Truth Statements. These examples show a method for restating generalizations made by ourselves or by other people. These sentences are not really quotations but generalizations about things that people say repeatedly. Verbs such as *believe, say, tell,* and *think* can be used for these general truth statements. Notice that the main verb is often in the simple present tense. Past time versions are also possible. The past time example suggests that the person's grandmother is dead. Present tense is used in the dependent clause because it is still true now.

present tense

My father **says** that my college education **is** important for our whole family.

I **want** to say that different methods of teaching **make** one college course more enjoyable than another.

Many people **believe** that an animal's life **is** as important as the life of a human being.

past tense

My grandmother **used to say** that it **is** better to teach people how to fish than to give them fish.

Reported Speech in Academic Writing

Exact Quotation. Academic writing often involves quotation of the words of others. Exact quotation requires the use of quotation marks. The source of the quotation must also be given.

The importance of telephone commmunication for modern government was illustrated by the comments of the president of the United States after a blizzard brought great damage to most of the eastern part of the country. President Bill Clinton was quoted in the Atlanta Journal (March 17, 1993, page A8) as saying, "I called a number of other governors yesterday. I'm going back now to get a situation report from the other states, and we'll process them all immediately."

Paraphrasing. Sometimes the information can be given in your own words. However, the source of the information must still be given. Using other people's information without giving them credit is called *plagiarism,* a very serious academic crime. Paraphrasing is difficult to do well. Inexperienced writers should avoid paraphrasing and should use exact quotation or indirect quotation.

```
The importance of the
telephone for modern
government was shown by the
telephone calls that
President Bill Clinton was
reported to have made to
several state governors
after a severe blizzard in
March, 1993 (Atlanta
Journal, March 17, 1993,
page A8).
```

Indirect quotation. This style makes some changes in the wording, does not use quotation marks, and provides a reference for the source of the information. The basic changes in the quotation include changes in the verbs and changes in the pronouns. Also, some words are added to indicate that the sentence is an indirect quotation.

```
The importance of telephone
commmunication for modern
government was illustrated
by the comments of the
president of the United
States after a blizzard
brought great damage to
most of the eastern part of
the country. President Bill
Clinton was quoted in the
Atlanta Journal (March 17,
1993, page A8) as saying
that he had called a number
of other governors on March
16. He also said that he
was going back to the White
House to get a situation
report from the other
states, and that he and his
staff would process those
reports immediately.
```

A Note on Changes in Verbs for Formal Indirect Quotation

In very formal contexts, the rules that are described in this section on indirect quotation are followed. However, these changes are not required by grammar rules but by a stylistic choice.

informal
```
A few months ago my
roommate told me that I am
her best friend.
```

formal
```
A few months ago my
roommate told me that I was
her best friend.
```

Even in formal contexts, these verb changes do not occur if they would change the meaning from that of the original quotation.

```
"If water is heated to 212
degrees F., it will boil."
```

possible but strange because it sounds hypothetical
```
My science teacher said
that if water was heated
to 212 degrees F., it
would boil.
```

better even for formal use because it keeps the original conditional meaning
```
My science teacher said
that if water is heated
to 212 degrees F., it
will boil.
```

Changes in Verbs in Formal Indirect Quotation: Sequence of Tense

Simple present tense becomes simple past tense.

```
"I speak Farsi and Arabic."

She said that she spoke
Farsi and Arabic.
```

Present perfect becomes past perfect.

```
"I have been to Paris at
least five times."

He said that he had been to
Paris at least five times.
```

Present progressive becomes past progressive.	"I **am planning** to go to Europe next summer."
	She said that she **was planning** to go to Europe next summer.
Present perfect progressive becomes past perfect progressive.	"I **have been studying** physics seriously for about twenty years."
	My physics teacher said that he **had been studying** physics seriously for about twenty years.

Changes in Modal Auxilary Verbs in Formal Indirect Quotation

Can becomes *could.*	"I **can play** the guitar."
	He said that he **could play** the guitar.
May becomes *might* for the meaning of "possibility."	"I **may go** to Europe next summer."
	She said that she **might go** to Europe next summer.
May becomes *could* for the meaning of "permission."	The teacher said, "You **may take** the test one day early."
	The teacher said that I **could take** the test one day early.
Will becomes *would.*	"I **will take** calculus and philosophy next year."
	She said that she **would take** calculus and philsophy next year.

35 **Sequence of Tense and Reported Speech** 227

Must becomes *had to.*		"You **must take** the make-up test tomorrow."
		My teacher said that I **had to take** the make-up test the next day.
Shall becomes *would* for the meaning of "future time."		"In this chapter, we **shall explain** the historical background of marketing."
		The authors of the textbook stated that in this chapter they **would explain** the historical background of marketing.

Pronouns in Direct and Indirect Quotations

Direct Pronoun Form	Indirect Pronoun Form	Examples
I	*he* or *she*	John said, "**I** am going to Canada for the summer."
me	*him* or *her*	
my	*his* or *her*	John said that **he** was going to Canada for the summer.
		John said, "**My brother** sold me this car."
		John said that **his brother** had sold **him** this car.

35

Direct Pronoun Form	Indirect Pronoun Form	Examples
we *us* *our*	*they* *them* *their*	Maria said to John, **"We** have to go to the library before class to get information for **our** project." Maria said that **they** had to go to the library before class to get information about **their** project.
you	*I*, *you*, or *we* *us*	plural *you* Our teacher said to our class, **"You** will have a test on this information." Our teacher said that **we** would have a test on this information. singular *you* Our teacher said to me, **"You** have to give your report next Monday." Our teacher said that **I** had to give my report next Monday.

35 **Sequence of Tense and Reported Speech**

☞ Practice 1

Analyze the following quotations for areas that need to be changed. Then, turn each into an indirect quotation for use in formal written English.

1. "I do the very best I know how—the very best I can; and I mean to keep doing so until the end." Abraham Lincoln quoted in *Six Months at the White House with Abraham Lincoln*, a book published in 1866 by Francis B. Carpenter.

2. "The man who dies rich dies disgraced." Andrew Carnegie in "Wealth," an article published in the *North American Review* (June 1889).

3. "I do not believe that civilization will be wiped out in a war fought with the atomic bomb." Albert Einstein in "Einstein on the Atomic Bomb," an article published in the *Atlantic Monthly* (November 1945).

4. "There is nothing I love as much as a good fight." Franklin Delano Roosevelt in an interview in the *New York Times* (January 22, 1911).

5. "Where I was born and where and how I have lived is unimportant. It is what I have done with where I have been that should be of interest." Georgia O'Keeffe in her autobiographical book titled *Georgia O'Keeffe* (1976).

☞ Practice 2

Practice making general truth quotations of things that people say. Complete the following sentences.

1. My mother often says that _____.

2. My father often says that _____.

3. My roommate frequently remarks that _____.

4. I believe that _____.

5. I think that _____.

6. Many people say that _____.

Other Units Related to This Topic

✔ **28.** Modal Auxiliary Verbs

✔ **34.** Present Perfect Verb Form

36

Subjunctive Verbs

Two Types of Subjunctive Verbs

Type 1. This subjunctive form refers to something that is **hypothetical** or **unreal.** The subjunctive expresses wishes, hopes, and doubts. Simple past tense is often used for this meaning; in this use, the simple past tense does not refer to past time.

I **wish** that I **spoke** French, but I have never had an opportunity to study that language.

Type 2. Subjunctive verbs are also often used in **formal communication about advice, recommendations,** and **commands.** For this meaning, the base or dictionary form of the verb is used.

When they talked last week, her adviser **recommended** that she **study** calculus next quarter.

I **urge** that each student **consider** the implications of an increase in tuition.

Verbs That Use the Subjunctive in Formal Communication

advise	*beg*	*direct*	*intend*	*propose*	*require*
arrange	*command*	*forbid*	*order*	*recommend*	*suggest*
ask	*demand*	*insist*	*prefer*	*request*	*urge*

Be and Subjunctive Sentences

In formal communication of subjunctive meaning, the infinitive form of *be* is used in statements about regulations and other types of requirements. Notice that the first example is about present time while the second example is about past time.

This quarter, our teacher **insists** that **students be** on time for all classes as well as for examinations.

Before the test began, our teacher **suggested** that **we be** especially careful in answering question number 10. That question was very complicated.

In formal communication of hypothetical meaning, *were* is used even where *was* would otherwise be used. In this meaning, past tense means that the statement is not true but is only a wish.

I **wish** that **he were** here to help us with this project, but he had to go to class.

Adjectives and Subjunctive Sentences

English can form subjunctive sentences that center on an adjective such as *essential, imperative, important, necessary,* or *vital.* Notice that these sentences use the following pattern: *It is (adjective) that (subject + base verb + rest of the sentence).*

It is vital that **each student be** on time for the test.

I think that it is imperative that **Maria talk** with her teacher.

Subjunctive Verbs

☞ Practice 1

Mark the noun clauses in the following sentences using square brackets [ ]; then, correct any incorrect subjunctive verb forms.

1. During our last class period, students taking English 101 classes visited our writing class and recommended that every ESL student keeps the *Longman Dictionary to* use in English 101.

2. They also recommended that every student writes at least one page in a writing journal every day.

3. Our teacher agreed with their recommendations and suggested that journal writing is turned in each Friday.

4. The students requested that their journals are counted as part of the final grade in the course.

5. Our teacher agreed to count the journal entries, but she also insisted that writing done in class counts more than journal writing.

☞ Practice 2

Complete each of the following sentences to explain your ideas on things that need to be done to achieve world peace.

1. It is essential that _____.

2. It is important that _____.

3. It is not necessary that _____.

4. I think that it is imperative that_____.

5. I believe that we should demand that _____.

Other Units Related to This Topic

✔13. Hypothetical Sentences

36 **Subjunctive Verbs** **233**

SECTION

XII

Punctuation

Commas

Using Commas Accurately

Commas are used for eight major purposes. It is important to understand that commas are used only inside sentences.

Rule 1: Commas are used with coordinating words to create compound and compound-complex sentences.

compound sentence

```
U.S. history is a required
course, but I would rather
take world history.
```

compound-complex sentence

```
U.S. history is a required
course that is especially
difficult for international
students, so I would rather
take world history if I
could.
```

Rule 2: Commas are used to mark the ends of introductory elements. When a dependent clause comes at the beginning of a sentence, a comma is used to mark the end of the clause. When a dependent clause comes at the end of a sentence, commas are generally not used to separate the clause from the rest of the sentence.

`Before Ana arrived in the` `U.S.,` `she studied in` `England.`

`Ana studied in England` `before she arrived in` `the U.S.`

`Before moving to Canada,` `Ali studied in England.`

`Ali studied in England` `before moving to Canada.`

Rule 3: Commas are used to separate items in a series. Most composition teachers require that writers place a comma after the next-to-the-last item in the list.

`English composition, U.S.` `history, and calculus` `are` `required for all students.`

`Writing an essay involves` `thinking, planning,` `drafting, revising,` `editing, typing, and` `proofreading.`

An Exception to Rule 3: However, in some situations, the last comma is not used. For example, in journalism courses and in newspaper writing, the last comma is never used in a series. You should be consistent in your use of commas to separate items in a series. Find out the preferred style for the courses you are taking, and use that style consistently in the writing you do for each course.

`English composition, U.S.` `history and calculus` `are` `required for all students.`

`Writing an essay involves` `thinking, planning,` `drafting, revising,` `editing, typing, and` `proofreading.`

Rule 4: Commas are used between the parts that make up dates and addresses as in these examples. Notice that a comma comes after the name of the country or the state when both city/country or city/state are given inside a sentence.

`She arrived here from` `Edinburgh, Scotland,` `on` `January 1,1990.`

`She arrived here on` `August` `30, 1990,` `to study at the` `university.`

37 **Commas**

Rule 5: Commas are used to indicate transitional words and expressions.

This university needs more computers for students to use. **For example,** I had to wait two hours for a terminal in the computer lab.

My brother took calculus in high school; **therefore,** he does not have to take it here at the university.

Rule 6: Commas are used to separate nonrestrictive relative clauses from the rest of the sentence. If the clause comes in the middle of a sentence, be sure to use two commas—one at the beginning of the clause and one at the end.

Popcorn, **which is a favorite snack in the U.S.,** was known to Native Americans before the arrival of the first Europeans.

George Washington, **who was the first President of the U.S.,** was also a wealthy businessman.

Rule 7: A comma is used to separate the tag from the rest of a tag question. Tag questions are not often used in writing.

Tuan is majoring in chemistry, **isn't he?**

Rule 8: Use commas in quotations when explaining who said the words. Notice that there are three ways to state such quotations.

He said, "I will take calculus next quarter."

"I will also take physics next quarter," he added.

"But," he continued, "I do not plan to take chemistry until the fall."

Problem 1

Separating a subject from its verb with a comma

Problem	Solution	Revision
★ Many people, like to dress in their cultural attire no matter where they are or what they are doing.	Commas are not used to separate subjects and verbs. Transition words and phrases can be inserted between a subject and a verb, but commas are not used alone in that position. Remove the comma, or add a transition word with a second comma.	Many people like to dress in their cultural attire no matter where they are or what they are doing. I do not like to wear my traditional clothing outside my country. Many people, however, like to dress in their cultural attire no matter where they are or what they are doing.
★ The most frequent worry that she has, is that she might not have money for tuition.	The subject of this sentence is a clause that ends with a verb. This combination puts two verbs side by side. However, a comma is not used to separate these verbs. Remove the comma. It is also possible to revise the sentence by using a phrase rather than a clause for the subject.	The most frequent worry that she has is that she might not have money for tuition. Her most frequent worry is that she might not have money for tuition.

37 **Commas**

★ Those who are badly hurt and cannot get the medical attention that they need, will die.	The subject of this sentence is a clause that ends with a verb. This combination puts two verbs side by side. However, a comma is not used to separate these verbs. Remove the comma. It is also possible to revise the sentence by using a phrase rather than a clause for the subject.	<u>Those who are badly hurt and cannot get the medical attention that they need will die</u>. <u>Those who are badly hurt and cannot get needed medical attention will die</u>.

Separating the parts of a compound verb

Problem	Solution	Revision
★ My older sister and I would clean the house, and get ready for school.	The example has a compound verb phrase. It is not a compound sentence. Remove the comma, or add a subject for the second verb. Compare the two correct sentences to see these two different solutions.	simple sentence with compound subject and compound verb My older sister and I would clean the house and get ready for school. compound sentence that combines two simple sentences My older sister and I would clean the house, and then we would get ready for school.
★ I went to school for two years, and earned my associate degree in data processing.	This sentence combines two verbs for a compound verb phrase—*went* and *earned*. Remove the comma.	I went to school for two years and earned my associate degree in data processing.

Problem 3

Separating parts of a compound noun phrase

Problem	Solution	Revision
★ War is bad for a country's foreign relationships, and its economy.	*And* is used to make a compound phrase—not a compound sentence. Remove the comma.	War is bad for a country's foreign relationships and its economy.

Problem 4

Separating a verb and its direct object

Problem	Solution	Revision
★ I believe, a person without knowledge of computers is at a big disadvantage.	The direct object of *believe* is a noun clause connected to the sentence with *that: I believe that* ...	I believe that a person without knowledge of computers is at a big disadvantage.
	That can also be left out. But, a comma must not be used. Remove the comma.	I believe a person without knowledge of computers is at a big disadvantage.
★ I remember, the results affected me psychologically.	This example illustrates the same problem. Remove the comma that separates the verb from its direct object.	I remember that the results affected me psychologically.
		I remember the results affected me psychologically.

37 **Commas**

Putting a comma in front of a subordinate clause or a prepositional phrase when it comes at the end of a sentence (except to show extreme contrast)

Problem	Solution	Revision
★ Success does not just come to people, unless they work hard and with determination.	This use of commas is not necessary and should be saved for special emphasis. Generally, no more than one or two of these uses should be included in any essay or paper.	Success does not just come to people unless they work hard and with determination.
★ I will buy a big house in the countryside, near a lake.	The writer does not need this comma because the sentence is not trying to emphasize the location of the house.	I will buy a big house in the countryside near a lake.

Putting a comma by itself at the beginning of a line

Problem	Solution	Revision
★ Good teachers prepare for class , and so do good students.	A comma must always be placed AFTER the material that it separates from the rest of the sentence. A comma never comes at the beginning of a line. Revise this sentence by moving the comma after the word *class*.	Good teachers prepare for class, and so do good students.

Commas  **37**

Problem 7

Avoid frequent use of a comma to substitute for *and* in compound phrases

Problem	Solution	Revision
☹ They make cars, machines.	This style can be used if the writer does not use it repeatedly. Generally, for academic writers it would be better to avoid this style. A compound phrase with only two parts should be made using *and*. A comma is used when the series has three or more parts.	They make cars and machines. They make cars, trucks, and machines.
☺ People learn reading, writing, mathematics in school.	This sentence would be improved by putting *and* between *writing* and *mathematics* to show that the series is coming to an end.	People learn reading, writing, and mathematics in school.

☞ **Practice 1**

Add or delete commas, where appropriate, to the following sentences.

1. Smoking has become a habit for many people, since it was first introduced.

2. Nicotine makes cigarette smoking addictive and when a person has developed the habit of smoking the body craves nicotine and wants more of it.

3. Also when a person has started smoking on a regular basis quitting is hard because the person has to change a habit.

4. Probably the most important reason why people smoke, is the relaxation and comfort that it gives.

5. However even if smoking is dangerous to one's health and annoying to non-smokers smoking will probably be a part of many people's lives because of one reason: it feels good.

37 **Commas**

☞ Practice 2

Add or delete commas, where appropriate, to the following sentences.

1. Many people like to spend their vacations at the beach the mountains or an amusement park.

2. Most amusement parks offer rides, and shows.

3. At Six Flags for example when you go on a ride you first begin to be afraid and then get really scared as if you are about to die but as soon as it is over you are still alive and well.

4. Although many of the rides look dangerous they are actually safely designed.

5. Free Fall for example brings visitors in a cart up to about five stories high, and then drops the cart down to the ground.

6. Many people feel great after each ride and there is always that spirit of adventure to try something, which they have never done before.

7. When people go to Disney World they are astonished to see Epcot Center which has amazing new-age products, and a beautifully constructed sphere.

8. In the Magic Kingdom where all the cartoon figures come to life and dance with you it is glamorous and fascinating to be part of a world where your fantasies come to life.

9. It is important to have fun during our vacations, because we need to get away from our daily schedules.

10. We however should realize that travel is not only fun but also a way to gain valuable knowledge.

☞ Practice 3

Two of these sentences are correct. Three have mistakes. Decide which sentences need to be edited, and make the corrections.

1. I did not quit school because I knew, I had to get a college degree to get a good job.

2. My father believed that all of his children had to get college degrees.

3. She remembered, her mother always encouraged all of her children to get college degrees.

4. We felt that getting a college degree, as difficult as it might be, was important in our lives.

5. The quality of self-discipline, is the foundation of a successful career.

Commas

☞ **Practice 4**

All of these sentences use *and* to make different types of combinations. Decide which sentences need to have commas, and add them.

1. You can learn physics **and** biology from books.

2. College is a place where students learn **and** grow both socially **and** intellectually.

3. College is supposed to be a place where students learn **and** where tests are used to measure that intellectual growth.

4. In factories, robots require less human labor **and** more computer technicians.

5. All college courses should provide both general knowledge **and** critical thinking skills.

6. The science requirements include physics, chemistry **and** biology.

7. John wants to be a lawyer **and** he is majoring in pre-law in college.

8. John wants to be a lawyer **and** is majoring in pre-law in college.

9. My parents went out of town on business **and** left me in charge of my brothers **and** sisters.

10. My parents went out of town on business **and** I was responsible for my brothers **and** sisters for one week.

Other Units Related to This Topic

 **Commas**

UNIT 38

Comma Splices

Definition of *Comma Splice*

Comma splice is the name for one type of mistake using commas. *Splice* means "to combine," as in combining two pieces of rope to make one piece. A comma cannot combine two or more sentences to make a new complete sentence.

★ My elder sister was like my mother, she tried very hard for me not to feel sad about not having a mother.

Ways to Correct Comma Splices

Revision 1: Separate Sentences. Make two separate sentences. Remove the comma; add a period at the end of the first sentence, and add a capital letter at the beginning of the second sentence.

My elder sister was like my mother. She tried very hard for me not to feel sad about not having a mother.

Revision 2: Add semicolon. If the sentences are closely related in meaning, use a semicolon rather than a comma.

My elder sister was like my mother; she tried very hard for me not to feel sad about not having a mother.

Revision 3: Add Coordinating Conjunction. If the sentences are closely related in meaning, add a coordinating conjunction, and keep the comma.

My elder sister was like my mother, and she tried very hard for me not to feel sad about not having a mother.

Revision 4: Use Subordination. Sometimes it is possible to use a subordinating conjunction to create a complex sentence. Such a change is not always easy because of the difficulty of finding the right word to go with the original meaning of the sentences.

problem

★ This university is not his, hers, or yours, it is ours, it belongs to all of us.

revision 1

This university is not his, hers, or yours; it is ours because it belongs to all of us.

revision 2

Because this university belongs to all of us, it is not his, hers, or yours; it is ours.

Problems with Comma Splices

Problem 1

Combining two sentences with a comma

Problem	Solution	Revision
★ My grandmother in Argentina used to joke about smoking, she said:"If God had wanted people to smoke cigarettes, He would have installed a chimney in our heads."	Writers have several choices for removing comma splices. In this example, the first sentence has been made into a separate sentence by deleting the comma and adding a period.	My grandmother in Argentina used to joke about smoking. She said: "If God had wanted people to smoke cigarettes, He would have installed a chimney in our heads."

★ Now people live busy lives, it seems to me that people are only concerned about their annual income.	This problem has been solved by adding *and* to create a compound sentence.	Now people live busy lives, and it seems to me that people are only concerned about their annual income.
★ Computers run factories, school systems, department stores, and other places, every part of a job seems to require computer skills.	This problem has been solved by substituting a semicolon for the comma at the end of the first sentence.	Computers run factories, school systems, department stores, and other places; every part of a job seems to require computer skills.

Problem 2

Trying to use a transition word as a coordinating conjunction

Problem	Solution	Revision
★ I am a nonsmoker, however, I believe that smokers have rights.	Some writers confuse transition words with coordinating conjunctions. Transition words cannot be used with a comma to combine two sentences; a semicolon must be used. Or, the two sentences must be made into completely separate sentences by using a period.	I am a nonsmoker; however, I believe that smokers have rights. I am a nonsmoker. However, I believe that smokers have rights.

★ First impressions are really important, however, we should not judge people by their clothes and physical appearance.

This writer has confused *however* with the coordinating conjunctions. The revisions show two ways to solve the problem. In the first example, a semicolon has been substituted for the comma at the end of the first sentence. In the second example, a period has been added at the end of the first sentence and a capital letter at the beginning of the second sentence to create two separate sentences.

First impressions are really important; however, we should not judge people by their clothes and physical appearance.

First impressions are really important. However, we should not judge people by their clothes and physical appearance.

★ Today, everything costs more, thus, economic factors lead people to have fewer children than in the past.

Another word that puzzles some writers is *thus*. *Thus* is a transition word and not a coordinating conjunction. The revisions show two ways to solve this problem.

Today, everything costs more; thus, economic factors lead people to have fewer children than in the past.

Today, everything costs more. Thus, economic factors lead people to have fewer children than in the past.

38 **Comma Splices**

☞ Practice 1

Correct the comma splices in the following sentences.

1. Living with my family has both advantages and disadvantages, most of them are advantages.

2. When we live with our families, we always have something to do, we can play with our brothers and sisters, talk with our parents, and get advice from our grandparents.

3. In contrast, if we live alone, we may be bored, we may have no one to talk to.

4. In my family, we help each other, for example, my older brother explains difficult math exercises and listens to my problems.

5. Because of these advantages, I would rather live with my family than live alone or live separately with a friend, I plan to live with my family until I get married.

☞ Practice 2

Each of these unrelated sentences has a comma splice. Find and correct the comma splices.

1. Take my father for example, he has never bought a pack of cigarettes in his life.

2. An educated person needs to know about many things other than the skills needed for a job, thus, college students should be required to take courses that are not specifically related to their careers.

3. People are sometimes judged by their outward appearance, however, their inner personalities are much more important.

☞ Practice 3

This sentence has five commas. Three of them are correct. One incorrect comma creates a comma splice. The other incorrect comma separates an adverbial from its sentence. Edit the commas to make the sentence correct.

I applied to a company, two years ago, the company rejected my application, but after I got my degree in data processing, the same company hired me, and I am working there as a data transcriber.

Other Units Related to This Topic

✔14. Coordinating Conjunctions

✔15. Compound Sentences

✔42. Semicolons

Comma Splices

Contractions

Words That Are Confused with Contractions

Each of the following sets of words is pronounced in the same way, but in written English, one is a contraction while the other is not.

Contraction	Not a Contraction
it's = it is **It's** a good idea to take a calculator to the calculus study group.	*its* The class will have **its** final examination next Friday afternoon.
who's = who is **Who's** going to the lab after class?	*whose* **Whose** dictionary is this?
there's = there is **There's** a requirement at this university that all international students have medical insurance.	*theirs* Here's my dictionary. Where did Juan and Marie put **theirs**?

Mehrdad and Kim are in the
library. **They're going** to
the computer lab at 4:30.

Mehrdad and Kim are in the
library. **Their** research
paper is due tomorrow.

Maria's teacher gave her
this note: "The mid-term
exam indicates that **you're**
having some trouble with
this material. Please make
an appointment to talk
with me."

Maria's teacher wrote this
note on her mid-term paper:
"**Your** answers are not quite
accurate. Plese make an
appointment so that we can
talk about what you can do
to improve before the final
examination."

Problems with Contractions

Problem 1

Confusing *Its* and *It's*

Problem	Solution	Revision
★ **Its** hard for many people to quit smoking because they are influenced by their friends.	Many people confuse the written forms of *its* and *it's* because they sound exactly the same in spoken English. In writing, *it's* is a contraction for *it has* or for *it is*. Revise the sentence by adding an apostrophe.	**It's** hard for many people to quit smoking because they are influenced by their friends.
★ The word <u>self-discipline</u> is not always defined to **it's** full meaning.	The writer needs to use the possessive form. Remove the apostrophe.	The word <u>self-discipline</u> is not always defined to **its** full meaning.

Problem 2

Using contractions when a more formal style is required

Problem	Solution	Revision
☹ Cheating doesn't benefit either the student or the school.	This sentence is grammatically correct. However, many teachers do not like for students to use contractions in written English. Find out your teacher's preference before you write a paper.	Cheating does not benefit either the student or the school.

☛ **Practice**

In the spaces provided below, write the full form for each of the contractions in the following phrases.

1. He wasn't _____

2. He's written _____

3. She'd eaten _____

4. I haven't driven _____

5. They won't attend _____

6. John can't speak _____

7. We'll travel _____

8. They've taken _____

9. They haven't taken _____

10. I don't understand _____

Fragments

Definition of *Fragment*

Fragment is the name for an incomplete written sentence. While we use fragments often in spoken English, they are generally not appropriate for academic writing.

spoken English

"You ready for class?" asked Petra.

problem in written English

*Because pollution damages their lungs. Many children in urban slums have health problems.

revision

Because pollution damages their lungs, many children in urban slums have health problems.

revision

Many children in urban slums have health problems because pollution damages their lungs.

Problem 1

Using a part of a sentence as a whole sentence (A complete sentence must have both a subject and a verb.)

Problem	Solution	Revision
★ Smoking in public encourages smokers to light their cigarettes in public places and creates a fire hazard. **Also allows them to smoke more cigarettes.**	This fragment does not have a subject. The writer needs to decide on a subject that fits this context. Several seem possible, including *this practice, this custom,* or *this law.*	Smoking in public encourages smokers to light their cigarettes in public places and creates a fire hazard. **This practice also allows them to smoke more cigarettes.**

Problem 2

Using a dependent clause as a separate sentence (An adverbial clause must be attached to a complete sentence.)

Problem	Solution	Revision
★ **When I compare the opportunities of North Americans with those of the people from the third world.** It is difficult to imagine how many people survive.	Adverbial clauses cannot stand alone, but must be part of a sentence. Substitute a comma for the period after *world,* and use a lowercase letter for *it.*	When I compare the opportunities of North Americans with those of the people from the third **world,** it is difficult to imagine how many people survive.

40 **Fragments**

255

★We cannot judge people by their appearance alone. **Because just from a person's looks you cannot tell if he or she is nice, intelligent, or stupid.**

Many writers have trouble with this type of fragment. We talk in phrases like these, but in writing the "*because* clause" must be attached to a sentence. Remove the period after *alone* and change the "*b*" in *because* to a lowercase letter.

We cannot judge people by their appearance **alone because** just from a person's looks you cannot tell if he or she is nice, intelligent, or stupid.

Problem 3

Using a prepositional phrase as a separate sentence (A prepositional phrase must be attached to a complete sentence.)

Problem	Solution	Revision
★My next project will be to invest a portion of my salary. **For my retirement.**	Remove the period after *salary*; use a lowercase letter in *for*.	My next project will be to invest a portion of my salary for my retirement.

Problem 4

Using a participle phrase as a separate sentence (This type of phrase must be attached to a complete sentence.)

Problem	Solution	Revision
★**Having the experience of living in a strange country.** A person can understand more about life back home.	Substitute a comma for the period after *country*, and use a lowercase letter for *a*.	Having the experience of living in a strange **country, a person** can understand more about life back home.

Creating a fragment by leaving part of the sentence unattached to the rest of the sentence.

Problem	Solution	Revision
★ Michael Jackson does not talk or dress like most men, but he is one of the top singers in the world. **And filthy rich.**	The writer wants to emphasize the last words in the sentence. In speaking, we would probably pause at the end before saying these word and would probably also say them with extra emphasis. The writer does not have those choices. The writer must find a way to emphasize the words while still attaching them to the rest of the sentence. (To emphasize part of a sentence, set it off with dashes or with a comma. A list can be separated from a sentence using a colon.)	Michael Jackson does not talk or dress like most men, but he is one of the top singers in the world--**and filthy rich.**
★ She has three children. **Michael, George, and Sarah.**	The writer wants to make the sentence more specific and interesting by giving the names of the children. The technical word for this type of addition is *appositive.* The more formal punctuation is to use either a colon or a comma. In less formal writing, a dash can be used.	She has three children: **Michael, George, and Sarah.** She has three children, **Michael, George, and Sarah.** She has three children-- **Michael, George, and Sarah.**

Fragments

257

Problem 6

Creating a fragment by separating an example from its sentence

Problem	Solution	Revision
★ Since I have been in the United States, I have learned many new skills. For example, driving a car and balancing a checkbook.	An example can be added to a generalization in at least two different styles. The example can be part of the basic statement. Or, the example can be a complete sentence. Both of these revisions are illustrated. Notice the difference in punctuation. In the first revision, the example is left as a phrase and combined with the sentence by using a comma. In the second revision, the example is made into a complete sentence by adding a subject and a verb.	example as part of a sentence Since I have been in the United States, I have learned many new skills, for example, driving a car and balancing a checkbook. example as a separate sentence Since I have been in the United States, I have learned many new skills. For example, I can drive a car and balance a checkbook.

☞ Practice

This writer has some interesting ideas and expresses them vividly, but her style is based on spoken English rather than on the complete sentences required by formal written English. Underline the fragments. Decide how they can be made part of one of the complete sentences with related meaning.

How Money Would Change My Life

¹If I won one million dollars, it would change my life in many ways. ²Once I had actually received the money, I would make donations to charitable causes. ³When I compare the opportunities in North America with those for people in the third world. ⁴It is difficult to imagine how we survived. ⁵If I should win one million dollars, I would use some to build schools. ⁶I would also donate money for uniforms, books, and meals. ⁷Remembering back then that many of my classmates were unable to attend school because they were lacking such items. ⁸My next project would be to build or maintain existing health clinics. ⁹Be sure that they are well staffed and equipped with modern

Fragments

equipment necessary to sustain and improve lives. [10] So often babies are dying because they are not immunized. [11] Because there are no available or nearby facilities to provide health care. [12] It would change my life to give an education to a brilliant child. [13] Who would otherwise end up washing clothes at the riverside for pennies a day. [14] Give life to a child who otherwise would have died. [15] Because there were no facilities nearby for treatment. [16] These things would bring satisfaction to me and change my life. [17] If I could change the lives of a few other people.

Other Units Related to This Topic

40 **Fragments**

Run-On Sentences

Recognizing Run-On Sentences

A *run-on sentence* is created when two or more sentences are written together without the correct punctuation. In problem #1, a new sentence begins with the word *it*. The sentence can be revised by making two separate sentences.

In problem #2, the comma has been left out that indicates that the sentence is a compound sentence. While many writers of English do not consider this an error, many teachers of writing courses consider the lack of the comma a serious error. Follow the style required by your instructor. The sentence can be revised by adding a comma.

problem #1

★ Economics 111 is very demanding it requires homework every day, quizzes each Friday, and five major tests.

revision #1

Economics 111 is very demanding. It requires homework every day, quizzes each Friday, and five major tests.

problem #2

★ Economics 111 is very demanding and many students avoid taking it.

revision #2

Economics 111 is very demanding, and many students avoid taking it.

Correcting Run-On Sentences

Choice 1. Add a period at the end of the first sentence and a capital letter at the beginning of the second.

```
Economics 111 is very
demanding. It requires
homework every day, quizzes
each Friday, and five major
tests.
```

Choice 2. Use a semicolon.

```
Economics 111 is very
demanding; it requires
homework every day, quizzes
each Friday, and five major
tests.
```

Choice 3. Change one of the sentences into a dependent clause.

```
Economics 111 is very
demanding because it
requires homework every
day, quizzes each Friday,
and five major tests.
```

Problems with Run-On Sentences

Problem 1

Not having a comma before a coordinating conjunction in a compound sentence

Problem	Solution	Revision
★ I am still working toward greater goals in my education but fame and fortune are nowhere in sight.	Some instructors require a comma before a coordinating conjunction in a compound sentence. Other instructors do not think that the comma is required but is optional. Find out the rule that is used by your instructor.	I am still working toward greater goals in my education, but fame and fortune are nowhere in sight.

Running two sentences together without any punctuation and without a conjunction

Problem	Solution	Revision
★ International students have an exciting way to improve their knowledge of the United States it is travel.	This sentence is actually made up of two independent sentences. To create one complete sentence, the writer will need to add punctuation and perhaps a conjunction. The writer could also choose to completely reorganize the sentence.	International students have an exciting way to improve their knowledge of the United States. It is travel.
		International students have an exciting way to improve their knowledge of the United States; it is travel.
		International students have an exciting way to improve their knowledge of the United States, and it is travel.
		Travel is an exciting way for international students to improve their knowledge of the United States.
		An exciting way for international students to improve their knowledge of the United States is travel.

Punctuate the following sentences correctly.

1. There are both advantages and disadvantages to living with family members rather than living alone I would rather live with my family.

2. When students live with their families they always have something to do they can play with brothers and sisters, talk with parents, and get advice from grandparents.

3. In contrast, when students live alone, they may become bored they may have no one to talk to.

4. In many families older brothers and sisters help younger brothers and sisters for example my older brother explains difficult exercises to me and listens to my problems.

5. Because of these advantages, I would rather live with my family than live alone I plan to live with my family until I get married.

☞ **Practice 2**

Correct the six run-on sentences in the following paragraph.

The Support of My Family

¹After living with my family for twenty-one years, I recently moved and experienced the feeling of being far away from my brothers and sisters. ²My brothers and sisters, even now, help me feel warm and not lonely they make me feel happy. ³I have eight brothers and sisters being a part of this large family, I have never felt lonely. ⁴When I was a child, my brothers and sisters helped me solve my problems today we often share our happiness or sadness by sending letters or by making phone calls. ⁵For example, my oldest sister helped me adjust after my move to college she still gives me advice about how to deal with problems that I have. ⁶Likewise, I enjoy helping my youngest sister and giving her advice. ⁷She sends me letters we talk on the telephone about twice a month. ⁸She tells me about her new friends and about how she is doing in school. ⁹Sometimes, I wonder how I would feel if I didn't have brothers and sisters. ¹⁰I think that the most important thing in life is being a part of a family I enjoy having many brothers and sisters.

Other Units Related to This Topic

41 Run-On Sentences 263

42

Semicolons

Using Semicolons

Semicolons are used to combine closely related sentences. They are used only within sentences. The first letter of the word following the semicolon is not capitalized unless it is a proper noun or some other word that is always capitalized. Semicolons are used sparingly. They cannot just be substituted for periods. They are best reserved for combinations when the relationships between the two sentences is so clear that a conjunction is not necessary. Overuse of semicolons is generally considered poor writing style primarily because the use of a conjunction makes the meaning of a combination more exact.

Rule 1. Semicolons can be used to combine sentences without using a joining word. That is, a semicolon can replace a comma and a coordinating conjunction.

without semicolon

```
Our English teacher
requires us to use a
particular dictionary, but
many students already own a
different kind.
```

with semicolon

```
Our English teacher
requires us to use a
particular dictionary; many
students already own a
different kind.
```

without semicolon

```
Calculus is required for
business majors, but
English majors do not have
to take it.
```

with semicolon

Calculus is required for business majors; English majors do not have to take it.

Rule 2. Semicolons are often used with transition words when two sentences are combined. Notice that these transition words are different from the coordinating conjunctions. This rule is the source of a great deal of confusion about the differences between commas and semicolons.

Our English teacher requires us to use a particular dictionary; **however,** many students already own a different kind.

Calculus is required for business majors; **on the other hand,** English majors do not have to take it.

Common Transition Words

also	*indeed*
first	*instead*
furthermore	*on the other hand*
however	*then*
in addition	*therefore*

Punctuation of Sentences with Transition Words

Rule 1. Use a semicolon to combine two independent sentences.

sentence 1

Calculus is required for business majors.

sentence 2

English majors do not have to take it.

combined sentence

Calculus is required for business majors; English majors do not have to take it.

42 **Semicolons**

Rule 2. Put the transition word at the beginning of the second sentence.

```
Calculus is required for
business majors; however,
English majors do not have
to take it.
```

Rule 3. Notice that a comma is required after the transition word.

```
Calculus is required for
business majors; on the
other hand, English majors
do not have to take it.
```

Rule 4. A writer can use transition words between two independent sentences. The first sentence ends with a period. The second sentence begins with a transition word that is followed by a comma.

```
Calculus is required for
business majors. However,
English majors do not have
to take it.
```

```
Calculus is required for
business majors. On the
other hand, English majors
do not have to take it.
```

Problems with Semicolons

Problem 1

Putting the semicolon at the beginning of a line

Problem	Solution	Revision
★ I have a degree in computer science ; however, I cannot repair computers.	Semicolons are placed at the end of a clause—not at the beginning. Move the semicolon to the end of the first clause in this compound sentence.	I have a degree in computer science; however, I cannot repair computers.

Using a semicolon where a comma is required

Problem	Solution	Revision
★ Because I failed the test, I thought I was a loser. **Later;** my father helped me regain my self-confidence.	The revisions show two possible solutions. Remove the semicolon, and use a comma. Or, remove the semicolon, and use no punctuation marks to separate the word *later* from the rest of the sentence.	Because I failed the test, I thought I was a loser. **Later,** my father helped me regain my self-confidence. Because I failed the test, I thought I was a loser. **Later** my father helped me regain my self-confidence.

Semicolons

Problem 3

Creating a comma splice by using a comma rather than a semicolon before a transition word to combine two sentences

Problem	Solution	Revision
★ People are often judged by their outer appearance, **however,** their inner personalities should be the focus of attention.	The writer has two choices: (1) end the first sentence with a period or (2) substitute a semicolon for the first comma.	People are often judged by their outer appearance. **However,** their inner personalities should be the focus of attention. People are often judged by their outer appearance; **however,** their inner personalities should be the focus of attention.

Using a capital letter for the first word after the semicolon

Problem	Solution	Revision
★ `There is one thing that most people agree on;` `It` `is our parents who teach us the most important lessons in life.`	Remember that the semicolon is inside the sentence and does not indicate that a new sentence has begun. The writer has two choices for the revision: (1) separate the two sentences by replacing the semicolon with a period, or (2) change the capital letter to a lower case letter in the word *it*.	`There is one thing that most people agree on.` `It` `is our parents who teach us the most important lessons in life.` `There is one thing that most people agree on;` `it` `is our parents who teach us the most important lessons in life.`

 **Practice**

Add, move, replace, or delete semicolons in the following sentences. One sentence is correct.

1. Using drugs is dangerous, drinking alcohol is also dangerous.

2. Many people believe that alcohol is not as dangerous as drugs, they are wrong.

3. Many lives are destroyed by drugs and alcohol, however, no one is trying hard enough to stop this serious problem.

4. I lived more than twenty years in my home country and felt very comfortable there, however; right now I am having problems adjusting to life in the United States.

5. Getting a driver's license in Japan is very difficult because of the required training and testing; however, it is easy in the United States.

6. I wish that I knew more about my culture and country because my friends here always ask questions about them however I do not know the answers to many of their questions.

7. I would like to learn more about the language, history, and culture of my country, nevertheless, I am happy to learn about the United States until I can return to Japan.

8. Computers are useful in schools, stores, and offices, even at home it is important to be able to use a computer.

9. Traveling gives us time away from our routines and gives us time to relax we, however, should realize that traveling also helps us gain valuable knowledge about other people and places.

10. In order to pass a test, some students cheat, though cheating is wrong; it should not be grounds for dismissal from college.

Other Units Related to This Topic

✔15. Compound Sentences

✔22. Complex Sentences and Sentence Combining

✔23. Subordinating Conjunctions and Types of Subordination

✔24. Making Transitions and Using Transition Words

✔37. Commas

✔38. Comma Splices

Problem/Solution Answer Key

UNIT 1   NOUN-PRONOUN AGREEMENT

Practice 1

2. a classmate: *he/she*
4. instructors: *their*
6. no problem
8. every student: *him/her, him/her*
10. a parent: *him/her, his/her children, his/her love*
    parents: *them/their children/their love*

Practice 2

2. *they, they*
4. *their*

Practice 3

2. ok but the pronoun reference of *they* is not entirely clear so it would be better to use a noun: *the management has installed*
   also possible: *small computers have been installed*
4. *his/her*
   also possible: *All people have their own personalities which affect their thinking, feelings, and behavior.*

UNIT 2   SUBJECT-VERB AGREEMENT

Practice 1

1. *There* is the subject, but subject-verb agreement is controlled by the word *categories.*
   there/are; who/go; who/go; who/want
2. *group/is, group/works*
4. *students/do*
6. *he/does*
8. *students/do*
10. no problem

Practice 2

2. *campus/consists*
4. *student/has*
6. *taking/helps*
8. *test/consists, essay/has*
10. no problem

UNIT 3   *A* AND *AN*

Practice 1

an angry customer   *a big house*   *an uninsured driver*
an unhappy student   *a holiday*   *a great deal of energy*

Practice 2
  2. no problem
  4. *learn vocabulary*

Practice 3
  2. no problem
  4. *a student*

Practice 4
  2. *an underground shopping mall*
  4. *a good*

UNIT 4   AVOIDING SEXIST LANGUAGE

  2. a parent: *his/her, he/she*
     parents: *their, they*
     [Note that the verb would have to be changed to match the plural parents: *If parents want their children. . . .*]
  4. an alternative to *cave man* is needed: *cave people, cave dwellers, people*
  6. *a professor: his/her*
     professors: their
     [Note that the verb would have to be changed to match the plural *professors: . . . if professors are biased about their students.*]
  8. an alternative to *chairman* is needed: *chair, chair person, department head*
  10. *a student: he/she is*
     students on student visas are: they are

UNIT 5   DEFINITE AND INDEFINITE MEANING FOR NOUNS AND ARTICLES

Practice 1
  2. *the homework for my writing class*
  4. no problem
  6. *The advice, the best advice*
  8. no problem
  10. *The computers, the writing lab*

Practice 2
The numbers refer to the sentence numbers in the paragraph. ◦
  2. *the United States*
  4. no problem
  6. no problem
  8. *the plane*
  10. no problem

Practice 3
The numbers refer to the sentence numbers in the paragraph.
  2. *the day*
  4. *the teacher, the ESL writing class*
     another choice: *my ESL writing class*
  6. no problem
  8. *the English language, the United States*

Practice 4

The numbers refer to the sentence numbers in the paragraph.

2. no problem
4. *the rest of my life, the future*
6. *the oldest granddaughter*
8. *the reasons*

UNIT 6 GENERIC MEANING FOR NOUNS AND ARTICLES

Practice 1

Answers will vary, but some examples of possible answers are given.

2. *Water is necessary for all life. I drink water with my meals. Water is basically a combination of hydrogen and oxygen.*
4. *I need a computer. A computer could improve my writing. A computer is a machine for doing calculations.*
6. *A student is a person who studies. I am a student. It is hard to be both a student and a parent.*
8. *Radios have changed life for people living in rural areas because they have brought the world to their farms and ranches. Radios provide news and music while television sets provide dramatic stories as well as news and music.*

Practice 2

Answers will vary.

Practice 3

The numbers refer to the sentence numbers in the paragraph.
Students and Tests

2. *These tests* is definite and refers back to sentence #1.
4. *counselors, seminars, students, tests*
6. *advice*

Edgar Allan Poe

1. *a poet, a short story writer*
2. *detective fiction*
4. no generic nouns

Water

2. *nature, ice, snow, water, steam*
4. *clouds, temperatures*

Used Cars

2. *used car dealers, large stickers, used vehicles*

Tigers

2. *tigers, subgroups*
4. *tigers, elephants*

UNIT 7 NONCOUNT NOUNS

Practice 1

2. *coffee,* noncount
   Coffee is a stimulant.

coffee, count (often in a plural form)
I had a coffee before class. ("a cup of coffee")
I had two coffees before class. ("two cups of coffee")
There are dozens of coffees grown around the world. ("dozens of types of coffee")
4. *homework*, noncount
6. *mathematics*, noncount
8. *advice*, noncount
10. *information*, noncount
12. *list*, count (*a list, two lists*)
14. *suggestion*, count (*a suggestion, two suggestions*)
I want to make a suggestion to my supervisor.
suggestion, noncount
Many people respond better to suggestion than to direct commands.
16. *government*, count (*a government, two governments*)
Representatives of the two governments met to discuss a trade agreement.
government, noncount
I am interested in the study of government. Government is as much a process as a structure.
18. *shirt*, count (*a shirt, two shirts*)
20. *computer*, count (*a computer, two computers*)
22. *course*, count (*a course, two courses*)
24. *vocabulary*, noncount
26. *equipment*, noncount
28. *politics*, noncount
30. *laboratory*, count (*a laboratory, two laboratories*)

Practice 2
2. *knowledge* (remove +*s*)
4. *vocabulary* (remove +*ies*, add *y*)

UNIT 8   NOUNS WITHOUT ARTICLES

Practice 1
2. *money, transportation*
4. *soccer, tennis*
6. *the work*
8. *classes, friends*
10. *college*

Practice 2
The numbers refer to the sentence numbers in the paragraph.
The noncount nouns are *news, information,* and *research.*
2. *the television set, places, programs, countries*
4. *programs, courses, experiments*
6. *a stressful day, a funny show, a classical music program*

Practice 3
The numbers refer to the sentence numbers in the paragraph.
2. *these disasters, accidents, accidents*
4. *the incidents, the consequences*
6. *disasters, the event, a relatively unpopulated area, the number of casualties, the incident*

Practice 4

The numbers refer to the sentence numbers in the paragraph.

  2. *cities, suburbs, a number of ways*

  4. This generalization can be made using either *the disparities/the differences* or
     disparities/differences. Notice the use of *population* as a count noun to refer
     to the two different "population groups."

*The growing socioeconomic disparities within metropolitan areas stand in sharp contrast to
the many decreasing socioeconomic differences between metropolitan and nonmetropolitan
populations during the 1970s.*

*Growing socioeconomic disparities within metropolitan areas stand in sharp contrast to many
decreasing socioeconomic differences between metropolitan and nonmetropolitan populations
during the 1970s.*

UNIT 9   IRREGULAR NOUN PLURALS

Practice 1

  2. *children*

  4. *lives*

  6. *mice*

  8. *series*

10. *teeth*

Practice 2

Answers will vary for the example sentences.

  2. *curriculums, curricula*

  4. *indexes, indices*

  6. *syllabuses, syllabi*

Practice 3

  2. *child*

  4. *wolf*

  6. *goose*

  8. *sheep*

10. *radius*

UNIT 10   PLURAL AND SINGULAR FORMS

Practice 1

  2. no change

  4. no change

  6. *many library books*

  8. no change

10. *two university teams*

12. no change

14. no change

16. *three classes*

18. *those college credits*

20. *four short stories*

Practice 2
2. *several months*
4. *my six friends*
6. *two essential characteristics*
8. *three rights*
10. *teachers, small groups, students*

UNIT 11 *THE*

Practice 1
2. *the Andes Mountains*
4. no change
6. no change
8. no change
10. *the Philippine Islands*
12. *the Sahara Desert*
14. *the Spanish language*
16. *the United States*
18. no change
20. no change

Practice 2
2. *The North of the United States, the South*
4. *the Far East, the Middle East*
6. *the Mediterranean Sea*
8. *the University of California, the University of Nevada*
10. *the Hawaiian Islands*

Practice 3
2. *The North Sea*
4. *Hawaii*
6. *The Erie Canal*
8. *Madrid*
10. *Switzerland*

UNIT 12 CONDITIONAL SENTENCES

Practice 1
Answers will vary. Possible answers are given as examples.
2. *If a student course evaluation shows a problem in a class, the teacher may need to choose a new textbook.*
4. *This university requires 550 on TOEFL. If a student makes 560 on TOEFL, s/he will be accepted.*
6. *If a student wears a business suit to class, s/he will be asked many questions by her/his friends.*

Practice 2
2. No problem
4. *will be forced*

Practice 3
2. *they may be successful*
4. *they can eventually suffer from lung cancer*

6. *the customers will receive*
8. *that student will face* or *that student faces*
10. No problem

Practice 4
Answers will vary.

UNIT 13   HYPOTHETICAL SENTENCES

Practice 1
2. *if I were rich*
4. *the first thing that I would do*

Practice 2
2. *if I had had money, I would have invested*
4. *I would learn, if I moved*
6. *I would like to have stayed, graduated*
8. *If I were*
10. *I would not be here in this college if I had won a lottery.*

Practice 3
The numbers refer to the sentence numbers in the paragraph.
2. No problem
4. *I would invest*
6. *The final thing that I would change would be*
8. *I would also be*
10. *I could be*

Practice 4
The writer uses simple present tense for general truth meaning in each of the five questions that s/he lists. The rest of the discussion is supposed to be hypothetical, but the writer was not consistent. Your task is to make changes to bring consistency to the hypothetical section of the passage. Also, there are some problems with the verbs in the general truth questions.
The numbers for the following answers refer to the sentence numbers in the paragraph.
2. *I would prepare*
4. No problem
Question #1:   *How well does the teacher know the material for the course?*
Question #4:   *Does the teacher really like the subject?*
6. No problem
8. No problem
10. *I would count and figure*
12. *This information would be of use*

UNIT 14 COORDINATING CONJUNCTIONS

Practice 2
Answers will vary. These are given as examples.
2. *and*   *I will cook dinner, and then I will study.*
4. *but*   *I have studied French, but I don't speak it.*
6. *yet*   *It is very cold outside, yet I want to go for a walk.*

Practice 3

Answers will vary. These are given as examples.

2. *My roommate likes rap while I like classical Indian music.*
4. *Because my physics teacher realized that we did not understand the problem, she gave us another example.*

UNIT 15   COMPOUND SENTENCES

Practice 1

2. Compound
4. Compound-complex
6. Simple
8. Complex
10. Complex (The sentence has a compound direct object with two noun clauses joined with *and;* the sentence itself is not compound.)

Practice 2

2. Compound
4. Compound-Complex
6. Compound
8. Compound-Complex
10. Complex (The adverbial clause has compound verb phrases, but the sentence itself is not compound.)

UNIT 16   GERUNDS

Practice 1

Example sentences will vary.

2. *enjoy* + gerund — *I enjoy listening to music.*
4. *hope* + infinite — *We hope to pass the physics test.*
6. *continue* + infinitive or gerund — *I continued to study even though I was tired. I continued studying even though I was tired.*
8. *manage* + infinitive — *I managed to get to class on time but I was almost late.*
10. *quit* + gerund — *I quit studying at 11 p.m.*
12. *prefer* + infinitive or gerund — *I prefer to study before dinner. I prefer studying before dinner.*
14. *imagine* + gerund — *I imagined passing the course without trouble but the final exam was really quite difficult.*
16. *try* + infinitive or gerund — *I tried to move the box. I tried moving the box.*
18. *recommend* + gerund — *I recommend studying in the library.*
20. *expect* + infinitive — *I expect to pass this course.*

Practice 2

2. *they start doing things*
4. *jogging and swimming*
6. *keeps telling me*
8. *began to learn* or *began learning*
10. *cannot help speaking*

Practice 3

2. *to cut*
4. *to buy*
6. *to build*
8. *saving*

UNIT 17   INFINITIVES

Practice 1
Example sentences will vary.
2. *imagine* + gerund	*Can you imagine living in France?*
4. *quit* + gerund	*I quit studying in the library.*
6. *hope* + infinitive	*I hope to get a good job.*
8. *recommend* + gerund	*My teacher recommends using an English-English dictionary.*
10. *continue* + infinitive or gerund	*We continued studying. We continued to study although the library was very hot.*
12. *afford* + infinitive	*Few students can afford to buy new cars.*
14. *enjoy* + gerund	*She seems to enjoy meeting new people.*
16. *postpone* + gerund	*Our teacher postponed returning our test papers.*
18. *prefer* + infinitive or gerund	*I prefer to study in the library. I prefer studying in the library.*
20. *manage* + infinitive	*We managed to find a good used car.*

Practice 2
2. *I will have to work*
4. *they hope to strike it rich*

Practice 3
2. *Since everybody was new to me, I also had to get to know people and had to introduce myself to the other workers.*
4. *The morning seemed very long and frustrating because I did not know how to do my job and because I felt uncomfortable.*
6. *The second day I returned to work with a smile, and I was ready to learn more about my new job.*

UNIT 18   OVERVIEW OF +*ING* WORDS

Practice
2. *boring*
4. *tired*
6. *rewarding*
8. *interesting*
10. *disappointed*
12. *frustrated*
14. *relaxed*
16. *fascinated*
18. *rewarded*
20. *confused*

UNIT 19   WRITING NUMBERS

Practice 1
2. *Two of her books and fifteen of her articles*
4. *February 16, five-minute report*

Practice 2
2. Two changes are possible: (1) *Fifteen thousand students completed the Student Opinion Survey last week.* (2) *Last week, 15,000 students completed the Student Opinion Survey.*
4. *between 9 a.m. and 1 p.m.* or *between 9:00 and 1:00*

Answer Key

UNIT 20   GRAMMATICAL AND LOGICAL PARALLELISM

Practice 1

2. *use the library efficiently or use the computer*
4. *to recognize this information and reduce smoking*
6. *want to get a good education and be*
8. *have loved and cared*
10. *to get into better colleges and have better jobs*

Practice 2

2. *dependability, determination, and self-discipline*
4. *because it is harmful to foreign relationships, the economy, and people*
6. *to make more friends, have a better attitude, and become adjusted*
8. *third, self-discipline is a characteristic of most successful people*
10. *Students can gain knowledge from educational institutions, such as schools and colleges, and from media, such as radio and television.*

Practice 3

Answers will vary. These are given as examples.
2. *yogurt and shredded wheat*
4. *students come from Venezuela, Saudi Arabia, and Somalia*

Practice 4

Answers will vary. This answer is given as an example.

   Cheating, one of the most common crimes in college, should be penalized for three reasons. First, tougher penalties like expulsion from college might stop potential cheaters. Second, cheating hurts all students. Finally, the most important reason is that punishment will help eliminate bad habits and will help students develop moral and academic standards.

UNIT 21   GRAMMAR AND USE OF PASSIVE SENTENCES

Practice 1

2. *it is listed*
4. *are stored*
6. *teacher lectures*
8. *was taught*

Practice 2

2. *can often be remembered*
4. *should be punished*
6. *should not be judged*
8. *could be changed* or *could have been changed*
9. *to acquire* or *to be acquired*
10. *have been hired*

UNIT 22   COMPLEX SENTENCES AND SENTENCE COMBINING

Practice 1

Answers will vary. These are given as examples.
2. *This language is a tonal language that has borrowed many words from Chinese.*
4. *In the seventeenth century, European missionaries developed a written language that used the Latin alphabet.*

6. *Although there are many differences between the languages, Quoc Ngu uses the same alphabet as the English language.*
8. *The Vietnamese language and the English language do not have the same word order; for example, Quoc Ngu does not place the adjective in front of the noun.*

Practice 2
The sentence type is given for the even-numbered sentences in the paragraph.
sentence 2:   complex
sentence 4:   simple
sentence 6:   compound
sentence 8:   simple
sentence 10:   complex

UNIT 23   SUBORDINATING CONJUNCTIONS AND TYPES OF SUBORDINATION

Practice 1
Answers will vary. These are given as examples.
2. *A student is a person who studies even if s/he is not in school.*
4. *A dictionary is a book that provides spelling, pronunciation, and meaning for the words of a language.*

Practice 2
Answers will vary. These are given as examples.
2. *I believe that hard work is not the same as smart work.*
4. *I am sure that all things will pass.*
6. *My teacher asked me why I had not selected the topic for my research paper yet.*

Practice 3
2. *I thought that learning English would be easy because I would live in the United States.*
4. *Although I studied hard, I did not receive the best grade in class.*
   I did not receive the best grade in class although I studied hard.
6. no problem
8. *I feel strongly that parents must guide the lives of their children because children do not understand many of the dangerous aspects of life.*
10. *Being good communicators in whom people can believe is important for all political leaders.*

Practice 4
Answers will vary. These are given as examples.
2. *The major languages of India belong to two language families, which are called Indo-European and Dravidian.*
4. *They include Hindi and Urdu, which is closely related to Hindi.*
6. *Dravidian languages are spoken by about 24 percent of the people who live in the southern part of India.*
8. *India's Constitution of 1950 identified Hindi as the official language of India while English was identified as the language for government and business.*

Practice 5
Answers may vary. These are given as examples.
2. *The student whose family lives in Paris speaks five languages.*
4. *The student was very angry because her textbooks were in the backpack which was stolen in the library.*
6. *The book, whose author lives in Mexico, won an international award.*

Practice 6

Sentence 2 has 1 relative clause and 1 noun clause.

Sentence 4 is a simple sentence with no subordinate clauses.

Sentence 6 is a compound sentence made of two independent clauses joined with a comma and the coordinating conjunction *and*.

Sentence 8 is a simple sentence with no subordinate clauses.

Sentence 10 has 1 noun clause.

Practice 7

In this passage, there are 11 adverbial clauses, 2 relative clauses, and 2 noun clauses.

Sentence 2 has 1 adverbial clause.

Sentence 4 has 1 adverbial clause.

Sentence 6 has 1 adverbial clause.

Sentence 8 has 1 noun clause.

Sentence 10 has 1 noun clause.

Sentence 12 has 1 adverbial clause.

UNIT 24   MAKING TRANSITIONS AND USING TRANSITION WORDS

Practice 1

2. This is a run-on sentence. It can be divided into two separate sentences, or punctuation can be added.

   Children do not have much experience or knowledge, and as a result parents must guide them carefully.

4. no problem

Practice 2

Answers may vary. These are given as examples.

2. *More and more companies are establishing non-smoking areas. In addition, they are hiring non-smokers.*

4. *In Korean culture, the oldest son has to take care of his parents, and I am the oldest son. As a result, I know that I will have responsibility for my parents when they are old.*

Practice 3

Answers will vary. This version is given as an example.

Leave out: *in conclusion* and *thus*. Keep *however* and *most importantly* because they emphasize two major points.

UNIT 25   FUTURE TIME WRITING

Practice 1

Notice that *will* is used two times while *be going to* is used once. Also, the writer uses some other future time phrases: *the rest of my life* and *toward my goal.*

Practice 2

The numbers refer to the sentence numbers in the paragraph.

2. *I believe that the person I will be after graduating from college will be distinctly different from the person I was when I entered college.*

4. no problem

6. *At college, I have met a variety of people from different countries, races, backgrounds, and religions.*

8. *This will affect the rest of my life because I will look for similarities in people instead of differences.*

10. no problem

12. no problem

14. no problem
16. *These traits will change the rest of my life by making me more capable of co-existing with other people in society and also by making me a more desirable employee.*

UNIT 26   GENERAL TRUTH AND GENERALIZATIONS: PRESENT TENSE

Practice 1
The numbers refer to the sentence numbers in the paragraph.
  2. *uses*
  4. *supply*
  6. no problem

Practice 2
The numbers refer to the sentence numbers in the paragraph.
  2. no use of *will*
  4. no use of *will*
  6. *Those in the second group take their jobs more seriously.*
  8. *They begin classes on time, and they try to make every class interesting.*
10. no use of *will*
12. *Teachers in this group make themselves available outside of class for students who need additional help.*
14. *Good teachers motivate and challenge their students.*
16. Because *will* is used for future time in this sentence, no change is possible.

UNIT 27   IRREGULAR VERBS
No answers needed for task.

UNIT 28   MODAL AUXILIARY VERBS

Practice 1
  2. *will be able to*
  4. *should have*
  6. *will be able to*
  8. *must send*
10. *might take*

Practice 2
  2. When I got tired of studying, I would think about my father's advice, and I would study again.
  4. Using this system, I could easily evaluate the performance of my teachers.
  6. In my home country if students wear clothes other than jeans, they must come from a rich family.
  8. During the storm, we lost all electricity in my neighborhood. All I could see was darkness.
10. If I won the lottery, there are three important ways in which my life would change.
12. If its leader does not know how to run an organization, it might be destroyed.
14. All elementary school teachers should have a bachelor's degree.

UNIT 29   MODAL AUXILIARIES FOR ADVICE, RECOMMENDATIONS, AND RULES

Practice 1
The numbers refer to the sentence numbers in the paragraph.
  2. no problem

4. no problem
6. *will advise*
8. *should follow*

Practice 2
2. *must keep*
4. *had better not eat, can cause*
6. no problem
8. no problem
10. no problem
12. *could live, ought to enjoy*

UNIT 30   MODAL AUXILIARIES FOR LOGICAL PROBABILITY AND FOR MAKING GUESSES

Practice
Answers will vary. These are given as examples.
2. *A neighbor might need some help.*
4. *He must be a foolish person and must also be greedy.*
6. *I could ask my teacher for permission to bring the paper the next day.*
8. *There MUST be a mistake. I will call the bank immediately.*
10. *He must work in the student health center.*

UNIT 31   MODAL AUXILIARIES AND PAST TIME WRITING

Practice
2. *should have taken*
4. no problem
6. *could see*
8. no problem
10. *could have been avoided*

UNIT 32   PAST TIME WRITING: PAST TENSE, PAST PERFECT, AND PAST PROGRESSIVE

Practice 1
The numbers refer to the sentence numbers in the paragraph.
2. *could enjoy*
4. *saw the Hawaiians make*
6. *were, were*
8. two choices:
   past time: *because it was a good place to visit, and everything was cheaper than at home*
   general truth: *because it is a good place to visit, and everything is cheaper than at home*

Practice 2
The numbers refer to the sentence numbers in the paragraph.
2. *While I worked there, I enjoyed my work very much.*
   While I was working there, I enjoyed my work very much.
4. no problem
6. *became, would not make*
8. *corrected, encouraged*
10. *I enjoyed myself very much while I worked there.*
    I enjoyed myself very much while I was working there.

Practice 3

The numbers refer to the sentence numbers in the paragraph.

2. *There were several adjustments that I had to make*
4. *When I looked for the Administration Building, I could not find it because it had been moved temporarily to another building while the offices were being renovated.*
6. no problem
8. no problem
10. *When I first saw my American classmates wearing shorts, I was embarrassed.*
12. *When I saw my classmates drinking soda or chewing gum, it was very surprising to me.*

Practice 4

The numbers refer to the sentence numbers in the paragraph.

2. *it was hard to understand what they said*
   or: *it was hard to understand what they were saying*
4. *I got angry*
6. *She taught me*
8. *Two years ago I was not able to understand spoken English because Americans, besides speaking very fast, used many difficult words.*
10. *now I can understand, because I spent*

UNIT 33   PRESENT TIME WRITING

Practice 1

2. *dislike,* usually used for stative meaning
4. *enjoy,* NOT usually used for stative meaning
6. *identify,* NOT usually used for stative meaning
8. *recognize,* usually used for stative meaning
10. *become,* NOT usually used for stative when it means "to change": *She is becoming tired because she is studying so much.* But, become is stative when it means "to make one look attractive": *That dress becomes you.*
12. *think* for the meaning of "have an opinion" is stative in sentences such as: *I think that she is a very good teacher.* But, *think* for the meaning of "consider, contemplate" is active in sentences such as: *I'm thinking about changing my major to political science.*

Practice 2

2. *knows*
4. *is taking*

Practice 3

2. *I use this object every day.*
4. no problem
6. no problem
8. *the important log button appears*
10. no problem

UNIT 34   PRESENT PERFECT VERB FORM

Practice 1

2. indefinite past/before now: *Compromises over the years have drastically changed*
4. definite past/over in the past: *After I graduated*
6. definite past/over in the past: *After I arrived*
8. indefinite past/not over yet: *has existed and has maintained*

Answer Key **AK.15**

Practice 2

Notice that the present perfect is used to conclude the paragraph. The writer first focuses on the past and then gives an indefinite past time conclusion—the conclusion is about the life of the writer—her life began in the past but is not yet finished.

2. *was*
4. *return* (Notice this is a parallel infinitive.)
6. *was*
8. *are* (Notice this is a general truth statement.)

Practice 3

The writer is still an accounting student, so the paragraph is about something that began in the past but continues now.

2. is (general truth)
4. *have taught*
6. *have built*

UNIT 35 SEQUENCE OF TENSE AND REPORTED SPEECH

Practice 1

Answers may vary depending on the meaning to be conveyed. Remember that a general truth statement may be given with simple present tense even when it is introduced by a past time verb form.

2. *In a magazine article published in 1899, Andrew Carnegie said that the man who dies rich dies disgraced.* (a general truth statement using simple present tense)
   In a magazine article published in 1899, Andrew Carnegie said that the man who died rich died disgraced. (follows sequence of tense but means the same thing as the first version)
4. *In 1911, Franklin Delano Roosevelt was quoted as saying that there was nothing he loved as much as a good fight.* (This is a personal statement that needs to be in the past because FDR is dead.)

Practice 2

Answers will vary. These are given as examples.

2. *My father often says that his family is the most important thing in a man's life.*
4. *I believe that human nature is basically violent.*
6. *Many people say that whoever dies with the most toys wins.*

UNIT 36 SUBJUNCTIVE VERBS

Practice 1

2. *They also recommended [that every student write at least one page in a writing journal every day].*
4. *The students requested [that their journals be counted as part of the final grade in the course.]*

Practice 2

Answers will vary. These are given as examples. Remember that the topic is "achieving world peace."

2. *It is important that each child be taught to recognize the dignity of all other human beings.*
4. *I think that it is imperative that each college student learn another language and visit a country where that language is spoken.*

UNIT 37   COMMAS

Practice 1
2. *Nicotine makes cigarette smoking addictive, and when a person has developed the habit of smoking, the body craves nicotine and wants more of it.*
4. *Probably the most important reason why people smoke is the relaxation and comfort that it gives.*

Practice 2
2. *Most amusement parks offer rides and shows.*
4. *Although many of the rides look dangerous, they are actually safely designed.*
6. *Many people feel great after each ride, and there is always that spirit of adventure to try something which they have never done before.*
8. *In the Magic Kingdom, where all the cartoon figures come to life and dance with you, it is glamorous and fascinating to be part of a world where your fantasies come to life.*
10. *We, however, should realize that travel is not only fun but also is a way to gain valuable knowledge.*

Practice 3
2. no problem
4. no problem
5. *The quality of self-discipline is the foundation of a successful career.*

Practice 4
2. no problem
4. no problem
6. *The science requirements include physics, chemistry, and biology.*
8. no problem
10. *My parents went out of town on business, and I was responsible for my brothers and sisters for one week.*

UNIT 38   COMMA SPLICES

Practice 1
Answers will vary. These are given as examples.
2. *When we live with our families, we always have something to do. We can play with our brothers and sisters, talk with our parents, and get advice from our grandparents.*
4. *In my family, we help each other; for example, my older brother explains difficult math problems and listens to my problems.*

Practice 2
Answers will vary. These are given as examples.
2. *An educated person needs to know about many things other than the skills needed for a job. Thus, college students should be required to take courses that are not specifically related to their careers.*

Practice 3
Answers will vary. These are given as examples.
I applied to a company two years ago. The company rejected my application, but after I got my degree in data processing, the same company hired me, and I am working there as a data transcriber.

UNIT 39   CONTRACTIONS

Practice

2. *he has written*
4. *I have not driven*
6. *John cannot speak*

8. *they have taken*
10. *I do not understand*

UNIT 40   FRAGMENTS

Practice

Sentences 3, 7, 9, 11, 13, 14, 15, and 17 are fragments.
Sentences 1, 2, 4, 5, 6, 8, 10, 12, and 16 are complete sentences. The errors can be corrected by combining the fragments with the other sentences or by creating complete sentences for the fragments.

UNIT 41   RUN-ON SENTENCES

Practice 1

2. *When students live with their families, they always have something to do. They can play with brothers and sisters, talk with parents, and get advice from grandparents.*
4. *In many families older brothers and sisters help young brothers and sisters. For example, my older brother explains difficult exercises to me and listens to my problems.*

Practice 2

The numbers refer to the sentence numbers in the paragraph. Answers may vary.

2. *My brothers and sisters, even now, help me feel warm and not lonely; they make me feel happy.*
4. *When I was a child, my brothers and sisters helped me solve my problems. Today we often share our happiness or sadness by sending letters or by making phone calls.*
6. no problem
8. no problem
10. *I think that the most important thing in life is being a part of a family, and I enjoy having many brothers and sisters.*

UNIT 42   SEMICOLONS

Answers will vary. These are given as examples.

2. *Many people believe that alcohol is not as dangerous as drugs; they are wrong.*
4. *I lived more than twenty years in my home country and felt very comfortable there; however, right now I am having problems adjusting to life in the United States.*
6. *I wish that I knew more about my culture and country because my friends here always ask questions about them; however, I do not know the answers to many of their questions.*
8. *Computers are useful in schools, stores, and offices; even at home it is important to be able to use a computer.*
10. *In order to pass a test, some students cheat; though cheating is wrong, it should not be grounds for dismissal from college.*